★ THE INTERNATIONAL ★

SPUD

Fun and Feast With the World's Favorite Tuber

Mara Reid Rogers ★ Photography by Mark Hill

LITTLE, BROWN AND COMPANY
BOSTON ★ TORONTO ★ LONDON

First edition

THE INTERNATIONAL SPUD
was conceived and produced by
Running Heads Incorporated
55 West 21 Street
New York, NY 10010

Editor: Rose K. Phillips
Managing Editor: Jill Hamilton
Production Manager: Peter J. McCulloch

ISBN 0-316-75412-9
Library of Congress Catalog Card Number: 91–58830
Library of Congress Cataloging-in-Publication information is available.

10 9 8 7 6 5 4 3 2 1

Published simultaneously in Canada by Little, Brown & Company
(Canada) Limited.

Printed in Singapore

DEDICATION

Often I am reminded of the message in Marcia Brown's folktale "The Stone Soup." The story is about three hungry soldiers who ask some villagers for food. The people refuse to share their food, each having a good reason. But the knowing and clever soldiers decide to make "stone soup." The villagers, very curious and anxious to glean the recipe, provide them with what they ask for, beginning with a "large iron pot," "many buckets of water," and "three round, smooth stones." The story unfolds with the soldiers hinting at other ingredients that would make the soup taste even better (yes, potatoes were among them!); strangely enough, the villagers suddenly found food to share. "A rich man's soup — and all from a few stones. It seemed like magic!"

This book is dedicated to the sharing of food, because as the villagers learned, you "shall never go hungry" if you "know how to make soup from stones," and as the three soldiers said: "It's all in knowing how."

ACKNOWLEDGMENTS

Many thanks to the entire crew at Running Heads, particularly Marta Hallett and Fran Obeid for sharing "the idea," and Rose Phillips for keeping it alive and well.

Also, to Little, Brown & Co. for its commitment to excellence, and a Happy 155th Birthday!

A zillion hugs and kisses to Mark, a talented photographer and "superhusband"!

★CONTENTS★

2
Baked and Roasted

Introduction

1
Boiled and Steamed

3
Mashed, Scalloped, and Au Gratin

4
Sautéed and Fried

INTRODUCTION

The potato is much more than a source of food. It has actually had an impact on worldwide social and economic events, thereby making its mark — or "potato-print," so to speak — on history. Were I to characterize the potato, I would call it proud. And certainly, as you shall soon read, it has the right to be so. The white potato, as we know it now, endures a romantic but difficult history: Its genesis was one of many transformations. It started as a simple tuber, became an esteemed symbol of prosperity, and later a lowly pauper. Luckily, although it took many lifetimes, the potato is now considered king, and rightly so, of all the cultivated vegetables.

Potatoes have existed since at least 3,000 BC. They were domesticated by the now legendary Incas of South America. The white potato began as a wild root ball deep in the ground of the Andes Mountains in Peru. The potato had proven itself an extremely hardy and tolerant tuber; the Incas grew potatoes at an altitude of 8,000 feet above where corn could prosper.

Imagine the Incas gathering potatoes amid the cold, wind-whipped mountains. And what a harvest it was! They had hundreds of varieties of wild potatoes, ranging in size from that of a grape to a grapefruit. Their potatoes also came in many shapes and textures, and the panoply of colors from white to orange, pink to purple, blue, green, brown and black. The Incas dedicated ceremonies to the potato and it became an object of worship and much pride. They felt the humble potato was a gift bestowed upon them. It was a secret, though, that they could not keep forever. After much trial and tribulation many, many years later, the potato would become a gift to the entire world.

Legend has it that in the sixteenth century Spanish explorers led by Pizarro in search of treasure plundered the Incas' silver mine and happened upon their potatoes — the true treasure! The potato, consequently, sailed back to Spain among the chests of other riches. However, from there the pages of the potato's scrapbook diverge. The common belief is that Spanish sailors had also been responsible for "discovering" the sweet potato and possibly the yam — two delicious types that are unrelated to each other or the white potato — even though *batata*, the Arawak Indian name for sweet potato, evolved into the English word "potato."

There are many theories and even more speculation as to how the potato traveled from Spain to the rest of the world — in particular, to European and North American dinner tables. One of the most popular beliefs is that the potato cargo of the Spanish sailors was later cultivated throughout the world's gardens simply because of its decorative flowers; the edible virtues were realized afterwards.

Though we do know that, through commerce, the potato made its way throughout Europe and to the British Isles there are numerous tales as to how it happened. It is suggested that in 1586, potatoes were transported on the ships of Sir Francis Drake to the Roanoke Island colony through something of a fluke. It seems that Sir Drake had been doing battle with Spaniards who had established outposts in the Caribbean. After successful warring, he was ready to return to England, but beforehand needed to stock up on provisions. He had heard that some of the British colonists on Roanoke were disgruntled and wanted to return home. Sir Drake made a stop in Colombia, South America, for supplies — among them, potatoes. As he picked up the colonists, he left some of his cargo in North America. He transported the rest of the potatoes back to England, where they slowly gained in popularity. It is thought that Sir Walter Raleigh was given some potatoes from this cargo, planted them on his estate in Ireland, and presented Queen Elizabeth with some choice specimens. Unfortunately her chef did not do the potato justice: He discarded the tubers but cooked the bitter leaves. Perhaps because of common errors such as this one in potato preparation, the spud's attributes remained largely unrealized in the European world from the sixteenth to the eighteenth centuries.

The people of the world were reluctant to accept the "lowly" potato because it was considered an evil and decadent food. They avoided the potato because it belonged to the nightshade plant family, and the potato plant was thought to closely resemble the poisonous European nightshade, known as the "Devil's herb." Another punitive mark was that the potato was not mentioned in the Bible, which immediately made it suspect as a wholesome food.

There were also many superstitions about the potato, such as the belief that if a pregnant woman were to eat one, her baby would be born with an abnormally small head. There were also many folk beliefs that it was connected to various physical maladies, among them leprosy and syphilis. The misconceptions were many, and the potato was in for a tough time.

The Irish, who were the first Westerners to grow potatoes as a staple carbohydrate, were devastated by the Irish Potato Famine in the 1840s. During this period, the potato was their main source of food. So when the potato blight caused huge crop losses, the six years of famine resulted in an estimated one million deaths. Needless to say, this event did not help the reputation of the potato.

Even though the potato played a part in

many people's diet, the white potato still had few friends well into the nineteenth century. Yet throughout history, it had influential supporters who believed in its culinary possibilities even when its reputation suffered from ill repute.

Among the potato's proponents was Frederick William I, King of Prussia, who believed that the potato was the answer to hunger among his subjects. In about 1720, he threatened to cut off the ears and noses of anyone who declined to farm spuds. Most of the peasants ignored his decree and, when he issued it again in 1750, they continued to disobey. The story goes that in desperation he ate potatoes on his palace balcony for all the world to see; his subjects then reconsidered the spud and decided that, if it was fit for a king, it was certainly good enough for them.

Another spud supporter was the French pharmacist Antoine-Auguste Parmentier, who also believed that the potato could help put an end to widespread hunger. He urged King Louis XVI to grant him use of land near Paris to farm potatoes. After raising a healthy crop, he had the king station royal guards around the field, his motivation being to entice the local peasants into stealing the valuable crops. Parmentier had the guards withdraw one night so that the peasants could take the potatoes. Thus began the process of the dissemination of the potato throughout France. Parmentier is the namesake of many traditional French potato dishes, including a soup and an omelet. He "marketed" the potato as a solution to France's intermittent famine. When the Academy of Besançon held a contest for the best "study of food substances capable of reducing the calamities of famine," Parmentier was the winner, because he touted the virtues of the potato so eloquently.

Stories of famous fêtes such as those in which he entertained Benjamin Franklin, among other important world-renowned political officials and the elite, with nothing to eat but potato-based dishes abound. At a court dinner which Parmentier "catered," Marie Antoinette was said to have worn potato flowers in her hair!

It wasn't until about the mid-nineteenth century that the potato received some of the tremendous respect it deserved around the world. It was recognized that not only would the potato grow well under poor conditions, but that it matured quickly, produced abundantly, could be harvested after sixty days, and stored well. The potato lends itself well to both commercial production and backyard plots, so it could be grown by the farmer and the cottager. Since the potato grows underground it could survive the trampling of soldiers in a war and the worst of Mother Nature's tantrums. Perhaps most important, people finally realized that the potato was also filling and delicious: you could eat one and feel satisfied.

By the end of the nineteenth century, the plight of the potato had changed for the better; the fears were forgotten, our hero had emerged a victor! The potato was a part of daily life, cookbooks had a multitude of recipes using potatoes, and roasted potatoes were sold by street vendors in American cities. The potato had arrived.

Today the potato is the most important vegetable crop in the world, and the third most important food crop. The power and popularity of the spud is well established. Potato consumption is very high in many countries, and the numbers are escalating. There are many rediscovered varieties of potatoes that now exist but, though they are reminiscent of the first Andean potatoes and their rainbow of colors, the potato has been improved upon and has more flavor and better resistance to disease than in bygone centuries.

THE INTERNATIONAL SPUD is a collection of recipes in which the potato is the star. The recipes I have created have been inspired by traditional ethnic potato and sweet potato preparations, or are evocative of a specific country and draw ingredients from its pantry. I have added my own personal touch to each recipe in an effort to make a healthy and delicious dish. For instance, I have added celery seed to the Jewish-American *Latkes* (page 108) for flavor and to replace excess salt. Ground cumin is among the seasonings used in *Shepherd's Pie with Orange-Potato Top-*

ping (page 52): though it isn't a traditional Scottish spice, it is tremendous with lamb.

I have tried to bring you a wide range of recipes, not only in their international scope and flavor, but in their various cookery methods and the time it takes to prepare them. All of the recipes are easy; some are rustic and "homey", others are elegant and appropriate for entertaining.

The potato is not only a nutritious, low-calorie vegetable that can be enjoyed year-round, it is an extremely versatile ingredient and can be served up in many guises. As you'll see in these pages, the potato can take the form of an appetizer, side-dish, condiment, main-course, or even dessert!

My hope is that, after trying some of the recipes, not only will your tastebuds be thrilled, but you will be as impressed and enthralled with the potato as I am. I have fallen in love with the potato in all its varieties, for it is far more than just a flavor. Its impact on cooking is far-ranging, whether it adds moistness to a bread, sweetness to a cake, or texture and stability to a dressing or sauce.

This book is a celebration of the potato for its place in history and for the inspiration and sustenance it continues to give. Suffice it to say, the motive was simple: What better way to pay tribute to the potato than by writing a cookbook!

— Mara Reid Rogers

Boiled and Steamed

1

Salad:

2 pounds small whole new
    potatoes, unpeeled, halved
    crosswise if large

1 medium red onion, very thinly
    sliced

1 medium yellow bell pepper,
    cored, seeded, and thinly
    sliced

1 medium red bell pepper or
    green bell pepper, cored,
    seeded, and thinly sliced

6 ounces feta cheese, rinsed,
    patted dry, and crumbled

2 medium ripe but firm
    tomatoes, seeded and cut into
    eighths

½ cup Greek Kalamata olives or
    other brine-cured olives,
    rinsed, pitted, and halved
    lengthwise

Dressing:

Makes 1 cup

½ cup fresh lemon juice

½ cup olive oil

2 cloves garlic, crushed

1½ tablespoons finely chopped
    fresh mint

1 tablespoon finely chopped
    fresh oregano

Salt and freshly ground pepper
    to taste

Anchovy fillets, rinsed and
    patted dry, to garnish
    (optional)

1. To prepare the salad: Place the potatoes directly on a rack or in a steamer basket in a 3-quart saucepan over 2 inches of boiling water (the water level should not touch the bottom of the rack). Cover the saucepan and steam for 10 to 15 minutes (depending on the size of the potatoes), or until they test tender when the center of the thickest potato is pierced with a fork. Discard the cooking water and drain the potatoes in a colander under cool running water. Let cool to room temperature.

2. Meanwhile, prepare the dressing: In a medium non-metal bowl whisk together the lemon juice, olive oil, garlic, mint, and oregano until well blended. Season with salt and pepper.

3. To assemble the salad: In a large non-metal bowl toss together the potatoes and half of the dressing and let the potatoes cool completely.

4. Add the red onion, bell peppers, feta cheese, tomatoes, and olives and the remaining dressing and gently toss until well combined. Garnish with the anchovy fillets if desired. Serve at room temperature or chilled.

GREEK-STYLE POTATO SALAD

(GREECE)

Serves 4 to 6

Dressing:
Makes 1 cup
¼ *cup white wine vinegar*
3 *tablespoons fresh lime juice*
½ *cup safflower or vegetable oil*
2 *cloves garlic, crushed*
½ *cup finely chopped red onion*
½ *teaspoon ground cumin*
½ *teaspoon chili powder*
¼ *teaspoon ground saffron*
   (optional, available at
   supermarket or gourmet store)
Salt and freshly ground pepper
   to taste
Salad:
5 *medium-sized boiling potatoes*
   (page 132), peeled and cut into
   ½-*inch-thick slices, then cut*
   with an octagonally shaped
   cookie cutter or other
   geometric shape, then boiled
   (page 136) just until tender
1 4-*ounce jar chopped pimientos,*
   drained (available at
   supermarket)
1 15-*ounce can black beans,*
   drained and rinsed
1 *ripe but firm medium avocado*

(CUBA)

Serves 4

1. To prepare the dressing: In a medium non-metal bowl whisk together the wine vinegar, lime juice, safflower oil, garlic, red onion, cumin, chili powder, and saffron until well blended. Season with salt and pepper.

2. To assemble the salad: In a large non-metal bowl toss together the potatoes and a third of the dressing and let the potatoes cool completely.

3. Add the pimientos and black beans and second third of the dressing and gently toss until well combined. Divide the salad among 4 salad plates, placing a neat mound of the salad in the center of each plate.

4. Cut the avocado in half lengthwise, remove the pit, and thinly slice each half lengthwise into 8 slices, a total of 16 slices. Gently, so as not to mush them, lay 4 avocado slices in an overlapping pattern to form a circle around the base of each salad. Drizzle the avocado with the remaining dressing and serve.

OTHER INTERNATIONAL POTATO SALADS

Toss each with your choice of dressing.

★ English-Style: Cooked, sliced potatoes with watercress leaves and crumbled Stilton cheese (English blue cheese). ★ Russian-Style: Cooked, sliced potatoes with thinly sliced cooked beets, sour cream, thinly sliced cucumber, and finely chopped onions. ★ Scandinavian-Style: Cooked, sliced potatoes with finely chopped fresh dill weed and slices of smoked salmon.

CUBAN-STYLE POTATO SALAD

4 cups homemade fish stock or
   4 8-ounce bottles clam juice
   (available at supermarket)
2 stalks fresh lemongrass
   (available at Thai specialty
   shop or gourmet store), thinly
   sliced and smashed with the
   back of a heavy frying pan or
   1 3-inch-long strip fresh lemon
   zest
3 kaffir lime leaves (available at
   Thai specialty shop or
   gourmet store) or 1 3-inch-
   long strip of fresh lime zest
⅛ teaspoon ground cayenne
   (red) pepper
3 medium-sized cooked boiling
   potatoes (page 132), peeled
   and cut into ½-inch dice
2 cups cooked fresh lobster meat,
   cut into 1-inch julienne or
   1 11.3-ounce package frozen
   cooked lobster meat, thawed
   and rinsed
3 scallions, including 3 inches of
   green part, thinly sliced
¼ cup canned unsweetened
   coconut milk, not canned
   cream of coconut (available at
   foreign section of supermarket
   or gourmet store)

1. In a nonreactive heavy 2-quart saucepan over medium-high heat, combine the fish stock, lemongrass, lime leaves, and cayenne and bring to a boil. Strain, discarding the lemongrass and lime leaves (or lemon zest and lime zest), and return the broth to the saucepan over low heat.

2. Stir the potatoes, lobster, and scallions into the broth and simmer for 5 to 7 minutes, stirring often, just until the potatoes are heated through. Remove the saucepan from the heat and transfer the broth to a nonreactive large heatproof bowl. Stir ½ cup of the hot mixture into the coconut milk in a small bowl, then stir this mixture back into the large bowl until well blended. Serve at once.

> "A man went out in his garden one day to dig some potatoes and sell them for pay. As he started to dig, one of them said, 'Well who in the world got you out of bed? For all this time you've let the weeds grow. Now here you come with your shovel and hoe. No thanks to you that at last I'm grown. Go away and leave me alone!' . . . Said the farmer, 'I heard my potato say, "Leave me alone! Go away!" And my dog stopped chewing on this bone and said, "You leave that potato alone!"'"
> —*Ennis Rees*, Potato Talk, *1969*

 OCONUT-SCENTED POTATO AND LOBSTER BISQUE

(THAILAND)
Serves 4, about 1¼
cups per serving

Gnocchi:

5 medium boiling potatoes,
   washed thoroughly and
   peeled

3 cloves garlic, halved
   lengthwise

1½ cups sifted all-purpose flour,
   plus more to knead dough

½ cup freshly grated Parmesan
   cheese

½ teaspoon salt

½ teaspoon freshly ground
   white pepper

⅓ cup firmly packed cooked
   fresh or thawed frozen
   spinach, drained, finely
   chopped, and squeezed dry

⅛ teaspoon ground nutmeg,
   preferably freshly grated

Butter to grease baking dish

Sauce:

Makes about 1½ cups

1 cup fresh or canned carrot
   juice (available at health food
   store), at room temperature

⅛ teaspoon ground nutmeg,
   preferably freshly grated

½ cup milk, at room
   temperature

Salt and freshly ground white
   pepper to taste

¼ cup Parmesan cheese
   shavings, to garnish
   (optional)

POTATO AND SPINACH GNOCCHI WITH CARROT-NUTMEG SAUCE

(ITALY)

*Serves 4, about
15 gnocchi each*

1. To prepare the *gnocchi*: Place the potatoes on a rack or in a steamer basket in a 3-quart saucepan over 2 inches of boiling water (the water level should not touch the bottom of the rack or basket). Add the halved garlic cloves to the water, cover the saucepan, and steam the potatoes for 30 to 40 minutes, or until they test done when the thickest part of a potato is pierced with a fork and is tender. Drain the potatoes in a colander, discarding the cooking water and garlic.

2. When the potatoes are cool enough to handle, but still warm, mash them with a potato ricer or potato masher until smooth. (*Note*: Do not use a food processor.) You will need 2½ cups firmly packed mashed potatoes.

3. On a lightly floured work surface make 2 mounds with the flour (each mound ¾ cup flour) and sprinkle each with ¼ cup Parmesan cheese, ¼ teaspoon salt, and ¼ teaspoon white pepper. In the center of each mound form a "well." Place 1¼ cups of the mashed potatoes in each well. Put the dry cooked spinach and the nutmeg in the center of only one of the wells. Gradually draw the flour into the first well, little by little, gently mixing it with the potatoes until the mixture is well blended. Gradually draw the flour into the potato and spinach, making a dough. You should now have two separate masses of dough, one plain potato, one spinach-potato. The dough should be slightly sticky.

4. Working quickly, on a lightly floured work surface knead each type of dough about 20 turns or until smooth. (The recipe can be made up to this point 1 day ahead. Wrap and refrigerate each dough separately.)

5. On a lightly floured work surface, break off several pieces of plain potato dough and, using your palms, roll each of the pieces into a 1-inch-thick rope. Slice each rope into ¼-inch-wide pieces, and roll each piece into a ball. Repeat the entire process with the spinach-potato dough. Carefully transfer the pieces to a baking sheet and lightly cover with plastic wrap.

6. To shape the *gnocchi*: Lightly dust your fingertips with flour. Using the side of a box grater with the small, raised perforations, gently roll a piece of plain dough from the top of the grater around in a "c" shaped motion, pushing your thumb into the center of the dough ball as you do so. You should now have a concave dumpling with a raised dot pattern. (*Note*: The center of each dumpling should be about the same thickness as the exterior, so that the dumplings cook evenly.) If the dough sticks to the grater, lightly dust the grater with flour. If the dough is too sticky to work with, gently blend some more flour into the dough. Repeat with the remaining plain potato dough, returning each dumpling to the tray when done. Then repeat the process with the spinach-potato dough. When all the *gnocchi* have been shaped, lightly re-cover them with the plastic

★ ALL EYES ON SPUDS ★
A Forecast of the Potato's Future

As of 1991, the USDA (U.S. Department of Agriculture) is in the process of trying to create high-quality potatoes called "super-spuds" by using "microtubers" (laboratory-reared potatoes that have been genetically engineered).

Alan Reed of Reed's Dairy Farm in Idaho has created Spudscream, an all-natural ice cream that contains 40 percent fewer calories than his regular ice cream. "Al & Reed's Sugar Free Ice Cream" is made with cream, milk, apple sweetener, and potato flakes and comes in a variety of flavors: chocolate, strawberry, raspberry, banana-berry, chocolate-almond, butter pecan, and vanilla.

Past inventions and those on the horizon:

★ Scientists at the Argonne National Laboratory in Illinois are developing a process to convert potato starch from potato peelings into bio- and photodegradable plastics. Will garbage bags be next?

★ The Ukrainian Academy of Sciences has carried out tests on a generator that uses potatoes as an electricity source. The scientists claim that a potato can produce electricity for almost a month.

★ J.R. Simplot of Idaho has produced ethanol from potatoes, which enhances octane and lowers the pollution level of gasoline. His scientists have also figured out a way to turn the potato sludge from making the ethanol into thrifty fish food.

★ The U.S. Department of Agriculture has created "Super Slurper," a powder made from potatoes that is able to absorb upon contact thousands of times its weight of liquid. Just think of the possibilities . . .

wrap and reserve at room temperature until they are ready to be cooked.

7. To a 6- to 8-quart pot of boiling water drop a single layer of plain potato *gnocchi* (about 10 to 12 per batch) at a time. Boil about 8 to 10 minutes, stirring gently once or twice to prevent *gnocchi* from sticking to one another or the bottom of the pot, or until they float to the surface. Using a slotted spoon, remove the batch of *gnocchi*, drain well, and transfer to a large shallow lightly buttered baking dish. Do not layer the *gnocchi*, or let them touch each other. Repeat the process with the remaining plain potato *gnocchi*, then repeat with the spinach-potato *gnocchi*, adding each batch to the serving dish as they are done, perhaps mixing batches so that guests can have some of each on their plates.

8. Lightly cover the dish with aluminum foil, and keep warm in a very low oven until ready to serve.

9. Meanwhile, prepare the sauce: In a medium non-metal bowl whisk together the carrot juice, nutmeg, and milk until well blended. (*Note:* The sauce will have the consistency of a dressing.) Season to taste with salt and pepper.

10. To serve, divide the *gnocchi* among 4 plates (be sure to include both types of *gnocchi* on each plate), drizzle with the sauce (the heat of the *gnocchi* will warm the sauce), and garnish with the Parmesan shavings if desired.

STEAK AND POTATO SALAD WITH CAPERS

(UNITED STATES)

Serves 6

2 pounds small whole red and white new potatoes, unpeeled and halved if large

½ cup malt vinegar (available at supermarket) or red wine vinegar

1 tablespoon sugar

¼ cup finely chopped fresh basil, plus 2 whole leaves, to garnish

2 tablespoons finely chopped fresh oregano or 2 teaspoons dried, crumbled

½ teaspoon salt

½ teaspoon freshly ground pepper

1 cup olive oil

¼ cup drained capers, rinsed

1 1-pound boneless sirloin steak, grilled or broiled to desired doneness, cut into ¼-inch-thick slices

4 hard-cooked eggs, thinly sliced, to garnish

1. Place the potatoes directly on a rack or in a steamer basket in a 3-quart saucepan over 2 inches of boiling water (the water level should not touch the bottom of the rack). Cover the saucepan and steam for 10 to 25 minutes (depending on the size of the potatoes) or until they test tender. Discard the cooking water, and drain the potatoes in a colander under cold running water.

2. In a medium non-metal bowl whisk together the vinegar, sugar, basil, oregano, salt, and pepper until well blended. Gradually pour in the olive oil in a slow, steady stream, whisking until the oil is completely incorporated and emulsified. Adjust seasoning to taste.

3. In a large non-metal bowl gently toss together the potatoes, the dressing, and capers.

4. To serve, mound the salad in the center of a platter, and surround with overlapping steak slices. Arrange an overlapping ring of egg slices around the edge of the platter around the steak. Decoratively arrange the whole basil leaves on the potato salad and serve.

> *"Be eating one potato, peeling a second, have a third in your fist, and your eye on a fourth."*
>
> *—Advice of an old man to a young man at the dinner table (an old Irish saying)*

5 medium boiling potatoes,
   washed thoroughly and
   peeled

1 medium yellow onion, finely
   chopped

6 slices white bread, crusts
   removed and cut into ½-inch
   dice

4 ribs celery, finely chopped,
   leaves included

12 ounces red or green seedless
   grapes, washed thoroughly,
   dried, and halved lengthwise

1 12-ounce can peeled whole
   chestnuts (brine-packed),
   drained, rinsed, and finely
   chopped (available at
   supermarket or gourmet store)

2 tablespoons unsalted butter,
   melted

2 teaspoons finely chopped fresh
   sage or 1 teaspoon ground
   sage

½ teaspoon salt

1 teaspoon freshly ground
   pepper

1 cup homemade beef stock or
   canned low-sodium beef broth

1. Place the potatoes directly on a rack or in a steamer basket in a 3-quart saucepan over 2 inches of boiling water (the water level should not touch the bottom of the rack). Cover the saucepan and steam the potatoes for 30 to 40 minutes or until they test done when the thickest part is pierced with a fork and is tender. Drain the potatoes in a colander, discarding the cooking water. When the potatoes are cool enough to handle, cut them into ½-inch dice.

2. In a large bowl combine the onion, bread, celery, grapes, chestnuts, melted butter, sage, salt, and pepper. Then add the diced potatoes and stock and using your hands gently toss together (so as not to break the potatoes) until well blended. Let cool completely before stuffing the poultry. Stuff poultry and roast as usual. Or bake the stuffing separately in an uncovered casserole, until heated through and lightly browned. (*Note:* Do not store raw or cooked stuffing in cavity of poultry. After serving, transfer any stuffing remaining in the cavity to a container, cover, and refrigerate up to 2 days.)

> *"No man can be wise
> on an empty stomach."*
> —George Eliot

Makes about 11 cups, enough to fill
the cavity of a 8- to 10-pound duck,
goose, chicken, or turkey

POTATO-CHESTNUT STUFFING WITH SAGE

(UNITED STATES)

Pasta:

Makes ¾ pound (Or substitute 2 sheets, total of ¾ pound, of fresh egg pasta dough)

2 cups sifted all-purpose flour, plus more if needed

3 large eggs, lightly beaten

1 large egg, lightly beaten, to seal

Filling:

1 teaspoon olive oil or safflower oil

½ cup pignoli *(pine nuts) (available at supermarket or gourmet store)*

1½ cups firmly packed smooth mashed potatoes (page 139)

1 large egg, lightly beaten

2 cloves garlic, crushed

1 tablespoon finely chopped fresh marjoram or finely chopped fresh oregano

2 tablespoons finely chopped fresh chives

Salt and freshly ground pepper to taste

PINE NUT-POTATO RAVIOLI WITH PUMPKIN SAUCE
(ITALY)

Serves 4, 6 2¼-inch ravioli per serving

1. To prepare the pasta: Sift the flour into a mound on a work surface, and make a well in the center. Pour the 3 beaten eggs into the well. Using your fingertips or a fork, mix the flour and eggs together until the dough begins to form a rough mass. If the dough is too sticky to handle, add some more flour. Using a pastry scraper scrape the work surface, preventing the dough from spreading.

2. Gather the dough into a ball and knead about 5 minutes or until the dough is smooth and satiny, adding a little flour if needed. Divide the dough into 2 equal parts and form each into a flat disk. Wrap each disk tightly in plastic wrap, and refrigerate for 1 hour. (The pasta dough can be refrigerated up to 1 day. Return to room temperature, but keep wrapped before proceeding with the recipe.)

3. To prepare the filling: In a heavy small skillet over medium-low heat, heat the olive oil. Add the pine nuts and cook, stirring constantly, for about 3 to 4 minutes, or until evenly toasted a light golden brown. (Be careful not to overcook or the pine nuts will be bitter.) Immediately transfer to a paper towel-lined plate to drain.

4. In a medium bowl combine the mashed potatoes, egg, garlic, marjoram, and chives and mix until well blended. Season with salt and pepper and gently stir in ¼ cup of the pine nuts, reserving the remaining ¼ cup pine nuts for garnish. Cover and refrigerate until ready to use.

5. To prepare the sauce: Force the pumpkin purée through a food mill fitted with a fine blade set over a small heavy saucepan until smooth. Whisk in the stock, olive oil, and season with salt and pepper to taste. Reserve at room temperature until ready to serve. (The sauce can be prepared up to 1 day ahead. Cover and refrigerate. Bring to room temperature before serving.)

6. To assemble the ravioli: Set the rollers of a manual pasta machine to the most open position. Feed the first disk through the machine while cranking. Fold the dough in half lengthwise and repeat. Repeat this process, folding the dough in half widthwise. Continue until dough is smooth and elastic. Wrap the first sheet in plastic wrap and repeat with the second disk.

7. Beginning with the widest setting, roll out the first pasta sheet, once through each setting, down to the thinnest setting. Trim to two 6-by-15-inch rectangles. Cover with waxed paper and damp paper towels, roll in plastic wrap, and refrigerate. Repeat with the second pasta sheet.

8. Working with one set of sheets at a time, brush one sheet with a quarter of the beaten egg. Working quickly, place 1 heaping teaspoon of the filling on the egg-washed sheet, placing the filling in 2 rows of 6 mounds, 1 inch apart and 1 inch from each edge of the pasta sheet. Lightly brush the second sheet of pasta with ¼ of the beaten egg and lay the sheet wet side down over the rows of filling. Press the sheets together to seal the ravioli. You will have 12 ravioli.

9. Using a fluted pastry wheel, cookie cutter, or knife, cut 2¼-inch wide circles or squares. Transfer to a baking sheet lightly dusted with flour and reserve. Repeat with second set of sheets and filling until you have 24 ravioli.

10. In a heavy 8- to 10-quart pot over high heat, bring 5 quarts of water to a boil. Meanwhile, place the saucepan with pumpkin sauce over low heat, and heat gently, while whisking occasionally, until ready to serve.

11. Drop in the ravioli and gently stir once. Bring to a second boil and boil for 4 to 6 minutes. Drain; divide ravioli, sauce, and pine nuts among 4 plates.

Sauce:
Makes 1 cup (Or substitute 1 cup homemade tomato sauce.)
12 ounces puréed cooked fresh pumpkin or squash or 1 12-ounce package thawed frozen puréed cooked pumpkin or squash

¼ cup chicken stock, preferably homemade, or canned low-sodium chicken broth
1 teaspoon olive oil, preferably extra virgin
Salt and freshly ground white pepper to taste

27

POTATO-ASPARAGUS FRITTATA

(ITALY)

Serves 2

Filling:

1 tablespoon olive oil, plus more
    if needed
2 cloves garlic, crushed
1 small yellow onion, coarsely
    chopped
4 ounces asparagus spears,
    steamed until crisp-tender and
    cut lengthwise into 1-inch
    pieces
¼ cup finely chopped red bell
    pepper
¼ cup brine-cured olives,
    preferably Greek Kalamata,
    pitted and halved lengthwise
1 cup thinly sliced cooked
    boiling potatoes (page 133)
1½ teaspoons finely chopped
    fresh marjoram or 1 teaspoon
    dried, crumbled

Frittata:

4 large eggs
Salt and freshly ground pepper
    to taste
3 tablespoons shredded part
   skim-milk mozzarella

1. To prepare the filling: In a 10-inch ovenproof skillet over low heat, combine the olive oil, garlic, and onion. Cook, stirring frequently, 2 or 3 minutes, or until the onion has softened. Add the asparagus, bell pepper, olives, potatoes, and marjoram, adding more olive oil as needed to coat the vegetables. Raise the heat to high and sauté the vegetables, stirring frequently, about 3 minutes, or until the asparagus is fully tender. Remove the skillet from the heat, cover, and set aside at room temperature until ready to use.

2. Preheat the oven to 325°F.

3. To prepare the frittata: In a medium bowl whisk together the eggs, 1 tablespoon water, and a pinch of salt until well blended. Add the mozzarella and whisk until combined. Pour the egg mixture evenly over the vegetables in the pan.

4. Bake, uncovered, for 15 to 20 minutes or just until the eggs are set but not browned. Season with salt and pepper. Loosen the omelet with a spatula and slide onto a warmed serving platter. Cut into wedges and serve at once.

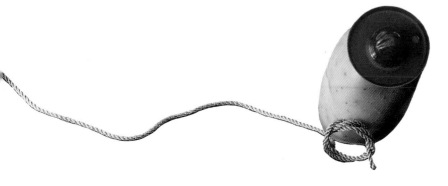

OTATO-CARAWAY SCONES

(ENGLAND)

*Makes 1 dozen
scones*

1 cup sifted all-purpose flour

½ cup freshly grated Parmesan
cheese

2 teaspoons double-acting
baking powder

1 teaspoon dry mustard

½ teaspoon salt

¼ teaspoon freshly ground black
pepper

¼ cup (½ stick) unsalted butter,
diced and chilled

2 tablespoons olive oil,
preferably extra virgin

1 large egg, lightly beaten

2 cloves garlic, crushed

1 tablespoon caraway seeds

¼ cup skim milk

2 cups ¼-inch dice cooked
boiling potatoes (page 136)

Lowfat "light" cream cheese, to
serve

1. Preheat the oven to 400°F.

2. In a large mixing bowl combine the flour, Parmesan, baking powder, dry mustard, salt, and pepper. With a fork or pastry blender cut the cold butter into the flour mixture until it resembles coarse crumbs. Stir in the olive oil, egg, garlic, caraway seeds, and milk until just blended. Gently fold in the diced potatoes to distribute evenly throughout the mixture, trying not to "mash" the potatoes.

3. Drop well-rounded tablespoonfuls of the mixture onto an ungreased baking sheet about 1 inch apart. Bake for 12 to 15 minutes, or until the edges are lightly golden. Serve warm with cream cheese for breakfast or to accompany soup or a main course.

★ SPUD STYLE OR POTATO ARTIFACTS ★

*A brief list of items that are either
in the shape of a potato or have
pictures of spuds on them:*

Postcards, burlap potato sacks (some converted to clothing), potato harvesting basket, souvenirs, cookie jars, toys such as Mr. Potato Head®, chinaware, pens, pencils, bookends, barrettes, buttons, jewelry, potato-based paint, postage stamps, potholders, candy, wallpaper, puzzles, placemats, napkins, stickers, hand lotion, stained-glass windows, make-up colors, shoes, Halloween potato costumes, stationery, shoes, furniture, and the list goes on . . .

1 medium tart red-skinned
   apple, such as Macoun,
   McIntosh, or Rome Beauty,
   peeled, cut into ½-inch dice,
   plus 4 more medium unpeeled
   tart red-skinned apples, ½
   inch from the top (including
   stem) cut off and base
   hollowed using a melon baller
   or spoon, leaving a ¼-inch-
   thick interior wall and bottom
   but not cutting through the
   bottom of the apples, to make
   4 edible containers with tops.
   Then rub the interior of each
   with the 1 tablespoon fresh
   lemon juice to help prevent
   discoloration.
1 tablespoon fresh lemon juice
1 medium boiling potato,
   washed thoroughly, peeled,
   and cut into ¼-inch dice
Salt and freshly ground pepper
   to taste
4 strips lean slab bacon,
   coarsely chopped
1 medium yellow onion, thinly
   sliced and separated into rings
Safflower oil or vegetable oil to
   grease
1 teaspoon Calvados (French
   apple cider brandy) or apple
   cider vinegar

1. In a heavy 2½- to 3-quart saucepan over medium-high heat, combine the diced apple, potato, and ⅓ cup water, and bring to a boil. Reduce the heat to low and cover the saucepan tightly. Simmer, stirring once, for 15 minutes or until the potatoes are tender but not falling apart. Season with salt and pepper.

2. In a large heavy skillet over medium-high heat, fry the bacon for 6 minutes or until browned and crisp. Using a slotted spoon, transfer the bacon to a paper towel–lined plate to drain. Carefully pour off all but 1 tablespoon of the bacon drippings and return the skillet with the drippings to medium heat and add the onion rings. Cook, stirring often, for 5 to 7 minutes or until golden brown.

3. Preheat the oven to 400°F. Lightly grease the bottom of a 9-inch square baking dish with safflower oil. Rub the outside of the 4 apple tops and bases with a little safflower oil and place the apple bases in the baking dish so that they stand upright. Reserve the tops.

4. Stir the bacon and onion rings along with the Calvados into the apple-potato mixture until well blended. Divide the mixture among the apples, firmly packing it down into each cavity. Replace the apple tops.

5. Bake for 15 to 20 minutes or until the apples are heated through. Serve hot. *Himmel und Erde* is a perfect side dish to baked ham, country sausages, or pork.

This Westphalian dish is composed of dense, unctuous potatoes—"earth"—and light, fluffy apples—"heaven"—hence its romantic name, which means heaven and earth.

 IMMEL UND ERDE (GERMANY)

Serves 4

SWEET POTATO ICE CREAM

(JAPAN)

Makes 1½ pints

1¾ cups milk

1¼ cups heavy cream

½ cup sugar

2 tablespoons freshly grated
 peeled gingerroot or 1
 tablespoon ground ginger

½ teaspoon ground cinnamon

½ teaspoon ground nutmeg,
 preferably freshly grated

4 large egg yolks, at room
 temperature

1 cup firmly packed smooth
 mashed sweet potatoes (page
 139), preferably variety labeled
 yams (page 135)

1 teaspoon pure vanilla extract

Cookies, preferably homemade,
 to garnish (optional)

1. In a heavy 3-quart saucepan over low heat, combine the milk, heavy cream, sugar, gingerroot, cinnamon, and nutmeg. Cook about 5 or 6 minutes, stirring often, or until the sugar dissolves and the mixture is heated through. Do not allow the mixture to boil. Let cool to room temperature.

2. In a medium bowl beat together the egg yolks and cooled milk mixture until well blended. Transfer to the top of a double boiler over barely simmering water and cook for 15 to 20 minutes, stirring constantly in a figure-8 motion, until the mixture has thickened and coats the back of a spoon. Do not allow the mixture to get too hot or boil, or the egg yolks will cook too much.

*"Here's taters hot, my little chaps
Now just lay out a copper,
I'm known up and down the Strand,
You won't find any hotter."*

—The cry of a London Potato Johnny during the Victorian Age

3. Remove the top of the double boiler from the heat and stir in the mashed sweet potatoes, a little at a time, until well blended. Using a fine-mesh sieve, strain the custard into a large bowl, forcing the mashed sweet potatoes through with a wooden spoon, leaving any fibrous material behind.

4. Stir the vanilla into the custard mixture and let cool to room temperature, stirring occasionally as it cools. (This recipe can be made up to this point 1 day ahead. Let cool, wrap, and refrigerate.)

5. Freeze in an ice-cream maker according to the manufacturer's directions To serve, scoop out and divide among bowls. Garnish with a cookie if desired. To store: Can be frozen up to 4 days only (to assure maximum freshness).

DESSERT DUMPLINGS WITH PRUNE-BUTTER FILLING AND APRICOT SAUCE

1. To prepare the dumplings: In a medium bowl mix together the mashed potatoes, egg yolks, salt, and cloves until well blended. Then using your fingers, blend in the flour until a smooth dough is formed. (*Note:* The dough will be sticky.) Remove the dough from the bowl, form into a flat disk, wrap, and refrigerate for 30 minutes.

2. To prepare the apricot sauce: In the bowl of a food processor fitted with a metal blade or in the container of a blender, process the drained apricots, lemon juice, and salt until puréed. Reserve until ready to use.

3. To prepare the prune butter: In a heavy 2- to 3-quart saucepan over medium-high heat, combine the chopped prunes, ½ cup water, the lemon juice, and lemon zest and bring to a boil. Reduce the heat to low and simmer, covered, for 25 to 30 minutes, stirring often, until the prunes begin to fall apart and form a purée. Transfer the prune butter to a small heatproof bowl and reserve until ready to use.

4. On a well-floured work surface, using well-floured finger-tips, roll the dough into 12 1½-inch balls. Using floured palms, flatten each ball into a 3-inch wide round. Repeat with each dough ball until you have 12 3-inch rounds and place them in between waxed paper sheets on a baking sheet. Reserve until ready to use.

Dumplings:
1½ cups firmly packed smooth
  mashed potatoes (page 139)
2 large egg yolks
1 teaspoon salt
⅛ teaspoon ground cloves
1½ cups sifted all-purpose flour,
  plus more to dust

Apricot Sauce:
Makes 1 cup sauce
1 16-ounce can apricot halves
  (packed in extra-light syrup),
  drained
1 tablespoon fresh lemon juice
Pinch salt

Prune Butter:
6 ounces dried pitted prunes,
  very finely chopped
1 tablespoon fresh lemon juice
1 teaspoon freshly grated lemon
  zest

(GERMANY)

Serves 4, 3 2-inch

dumplings each

5. In a 8- to 10-quart heavy pot bring 5 quarts of water to a boil. Pour ½ cup of the apricot sauce into a shallow baking dish. Preheat the oven to 150°F.

6. Meanwhile, place 2 teaspoonfuls of the prune butter in the center of each dough round and draw the edges of the dough together over it while pushing in the filling, pinching firmly to seal and form a ball. Remove and discard any excess dough where pinched to create an even layer of dough all around. Repeat with the remaining dough and prune butter until you have 12 dumplings.

7. Drop a single layer of dumplings (about 4 to 6 per batch) at a time into the boiling water. Stir gently once or twice to prevent them from sticking to one another or the bottom of the pot. Boil 7 to 9 minutes, or until they float to the surface. Using a slotted spoon, remove the batch of dumplings, drain in a colander, and transfer to the baking dish. Pour some of the apricot sauce over the dumplings, tossing gently to coat them evenly. Transfer the dish to the oven to keep warm in between batches. Repeat the process with the remaining dumplings, adding each batch to the serving dish as they are done and drizzling with apricot sauce.

8. To serve, divide the warm dumplings and sauce among 4 shallow soup bowls and serve at once.

Baked and Roasted

2

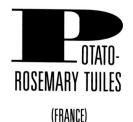

POTATO-ROSEMARY TUILES

(FRANCE)

Makes about 20 3-inch wafers

3 tablespoons unsalted butter, at
  room temperature, plus more
  to grease baking sheet
1 tablespoon confectioners' sugar
½ teaspoon salt
¼ cup firmly packed smooth
  mashed potato (page 139)
1 large egg white
½ cup sifted cake flour
2 teaspoons dried rosemary
2 tablespoons coarse (kosher)
  salt, to garnish

*"That which was here-
tofore reckon'd a food
fit only for Irishmen
and clowns is now
become the diet of
the most luxuriously
polite."*
—*Stephen Switzer,*
  Writing On Pota-
  toes, *1733*

1. Preheat the oven to 450°F. Place a rack in the middle of the oven. Lightly butter a baking sheet.

2. In a medium bowl beat together the 3 tablespoons butter, confectioners' sugar, the ½ teaspoon salt, and mashed potato until well blended. Add the egg white, beating only briefly, just until blended.

3. Sift the flour into the bowl with the potato mixture, and gently fold it in until well blended.

4. Working quickly, drop teaspoonfuls of dough about 3 inches apart on the buttered baking sheet. With the back of a spoon or rubber spatula, spread out each into a circle about 3 inches in diameter. (*Note:* The wafer should be even in thickness and not have any holes.) Sprinkle each circle with a pinch of rosemary and a pinch of coarse salt.

5. Bake for 5 to 7 minutes or until the edges are golden brown. Working quickly, using a thin spatula remove each wafer, and place it rosemary side up onto the rolling pin. Push it against the pin to "mold" the wafer into a curved shape. (*Note:* If the wafers crisp before you can mold them, return them to the oven for a few seconds to soften.) Transfer to a wire rack to finish cooling. Repeat with the remaining batter, regreasing the baking sheet in between batches if needed. Serve at once, as an hors d'oeuvre or accompaniment to a lamb, beef, poultry, or seafood main course.

POTATO PIROG

(Oval-Shaped Savory Pie)

(SOVIET UNION)

Serves 6

1. To prepare the dough: In a medium bowl cream together the butter and cream cheese until well blended and smooth. Beat in the sour cream just until well blended.

2. In a separate medium bowl sift together the flour, sugar, and salt until combined. Stir the flour mixture into the cream cheese mixture until well blended and a soft dough forms. Transfer the dough to a lightly floured work surface and knead 3 or 4 times or just until smooth. Divide the dough into two equal parts and form each into a flat disk. Wrap separately in waxed paper and refrigerate for 1 hour, preferably overnight.

Dough:

½ cup (1 stick) unsalted butter,
  at room temperature, plus
  more to grease

8 ounces cream cheese,
  preferably lowfat "light," at
  room temperature

¼ cup sour cream

2 cups sifted all-purpose flour,
  plus more to dust

1 teaspoon sugar

½ teaspoon salt

1 large egg beaten with 1
  tablespoon milk, to glaze

Filling:

2 cups firmly packed mashed
  potatoes (page 139)

4 ounces cream cheese,
  preferably lowfat "light," at
  room temperature

4 scallions, including 3 inches of
  green part, thinly sliced

½ cup freshly grated Parmesan
  cheese

½ teaspoon salt

¼ teaspoon freshly ground
  pepper

1 large egg yolk, lightly beaten

3. To prepare the filling: In a medium bowl mix together the mashed potatoes and cream cheese until well blended. Stir in the scallions, Parmesan cheese, salt, pepper, and egg yolk until well blended.

4. Let the dough return to room temperature before rolling. On a lightly floured work surface, using a well-floured rolling pin, roll out one piece of the dough to an oval about 12 inches long and 8 inches wide and a uniform ⅛-inch thickness. Transfer the dough to a lightly greased baking sheet. Repeat with the second dough disk, leaving it on the work surface until ready to use.

5. Spoon the potato filling in a 9-inch-long and 4-inch-wide mound down the center of the pastry on the baking sheet, leaving a 2-inch margin on the sides and a 2½-inch margin of dough at either end. Press gently down on the filling to mold it into a narrow, elongated shape. Using a pastry brush, paint some of the egg glaze along the edges of the filling. Lay the remaining sheet of pastry over the filling and press the edges of the dough together to encase the filling. Trim the edges of the pastry, leaving a 1-inch overhang, and crimp the edges to seal further. Use the extra pastry scraps to make decorations on the pastry, cutting them into designs with a knife or cookie cutter. Brush the surface of the pastry with the remaining egg glaze, sticking the pastry decorations on in a pleasing pattern. Cut a small ¼-inch-wide hole in the center of the pastry to allow steam to escape.

6. Preheat the oven to 425°F.

7. Bake the pastry for 30 to 40 minutes or until it is golden brown and sounds hollow when tapped. Serve at once.

1 pound extra-lean ground beef

1 medium yellow onion, minced

¼ cup firmly packed smooth
  mashed potatoes (page 139)

⅓ cup minced cooked fresh
  beets or minced drained
  canned beets

2 teaspoons truffle mustard or
  Dijon-style mustard

1 tablespoon finely chopped
  fresh tarragon or 2 teaspoons
  dried, crumbled

½ teaspoon freshly ground
  pepper

4 hard rolls, split and heated or
  toasted, to serve

Hamburger accompaniments:
  lettuce, tomato, cheese of your
  choice, relish, ketchup, and
  mustard, to serve

> "Potatoes, like wives,
> should never be taken
> for granted."
>
> —Peter Pirbright,
> Off The Beaten
> Track, *1946*

1. Preheat the grill or broiler.

2. To prepare the burgers: In a medium bowl gently stir together the beef, onion, mashed potatoes, beets, mustard, tarragon, and pepper until well blended. Shape into 4 flat 4-inch patties. Reserve at room temperature until ready to use.

3. For the grill: Over hot coals, grill the hamburgers about 5 inches from the coals, for 3 to 4 minutes per side for rare, 4 to 5 minutes per side for medium-rare, and 5 to 6 minutes per side for well done.

4. For the broiler: Broil about 4 to 5 inches from the heat, 4 to 5 minutes per side for rare, 5 to 6 minutes per side for medium-rare, and 6 to 7 minutes per side for well done. (*Note:* Grill and broiler times are approximate. Cook to desired doneness and remember that the meat will cook a little more even after it has been removed from the heat.)

5. To serve, assemble the hamburgers on rolls, and pass with the accompaniments, allowing the guests to help themselves.

SPUD-BURGERS DELUXE

(AUSTRALIA)

Serves 4

★ POTATO BY ANY OTHER NAME ★

Here are some alliterative translations of international spud terminology:

Solanum tuberosum (Latin)	*Aardappel* (Dutch)	*Patata* (Italian)
Kentang (Indonesian)	*Cartof* (Romanian)	*Kartoffel* (Danish)
Patata, tartuffo (Spanish)	*Pomme de terre* (French)	*Bulvė* (Lithuanian)
Kartoffel, erdapfel (German)	*Kartofel* (Russian)	

WEET POTATO VINE BISCUITS

(UNITED STATES)

Makes 2½ dozen 2-inch biscuits

2 cups sifted all-purpose flour,
   plus more to dust
2 teaspoons double-acting
   baking powder
½ teaspoon salt
¼ cup (½ stick) unsalted butter,
   diced and chilled
1 cup firmly packed mashed
   sweet potatoes (page 139),
   preferably variety labeled
   yams (page 133)
¼ cup milk
1 large egg beaten with 1
   tablespoon milk, to glaze
3 tablespoons coarsely chopped
   crystallized ginger (available
   at supermarket or gourmet
   store), to garnish

1. In a medium mixing bowl sift together the flour, baking powder, and salt. Using a pastry blender or fork, cut in the chilled butter until the mixture resembles coarse crumbs. Stir in the mashed sweet potatoes and milk until dough just clings together.

2. Preheat the oven to 450°F.

3. On a lightly floured work surface, knead the dough gently for 10 to 12 turns or until it is well blended and smooth. Using a lightly floured rolling pin, roll the dough uniformly out ¼ inch thick. Using a floured 2-inch biscuit cutter, cut the dough into rounds, dipping the cutter back into the flour between cuts when necessary. (*Note*: To insure straight-sided biscuits do not twist the biscuit cutter as you cut, or flatten the edges of the biscuits.) Reroll scraps of dough and repeat the process until you have 30 biscuits.

4. Transfer the biscuits to an ungreased baking sheet, placing them 1 inch apart. Brush the top of the biscuits lightly with the egg glaze and sprinkle the top of each with some of the crystallized ginger. Bake for 8 to 10 minutes or until the edges are very lightly browned. Serve at once.

2 medium eggplants, unpeeled
  and cut into 24 ½-inch-thick
  slices
2 large boiling potatoes, washed
  thoroughly, peeled, and cut
  into 12 ¼-inch-thick slices
Olive oil, to brush

Filling:
2 teaspoons olive oil, plus more
  to grease
1 medium yellow onion, finely
  chopped
2 cloves garlic, crushed
½ pound lean ground lamb
1 14½-ounce can peeled whole
  tomatoes, crushed and
  drained
¼ cup brandy
½ teaspoon ground allspice
2 teaspoons minced fresh
  oregano or 1 teaspoon dried,
  crumbled
Salt and freshly ground pepper
  to taste
1 8-ounce piece feta cheese, cut
  into 12 slices

1. Preheat the oven to 375°F.

2. Lightly brush both sides of the eggplant and the potato slices with olive oil and transfer to 3 or 4 shallow baking pans (large enough to accommodate the eggplant and potato slices in a single layer). Arrange the slices in a single layer among the baking pans. Bake for 25 to 30 minutes or until both the eggplant and potatoes test tender when pierced with a fork.

3. Meanwhile, prepare the filling: In a heavy large skillet over medium heat, heat the olive oil. Add the onion and garlic and cook, stirring, for 3 to 4 minutes or until the onion is soft but not browned. Add the lamb and cook, breaking up the meat with the back of a wooden spoon, until the meat browns, about 7 to 10 minutes. Carefully pour off excess fat.

4. Return the skillet to medium heat and stir in the drained crushed tomatoes, brandy, allspice, and oregano and season with salt and pepper. Reduce the heat to low and simmer for 18 to 20 minutes more, stirring occasionally, or until almost all the liquid has evaporated and the mixture has thickened. You should have about 1½ cups filling.

INDIVIDUAL POTATO MOUSSAKA

(GREECE)
Serves 6,
2 per serving

Topping:
Makes 2 cups
6 tablespoons unsalted butter
6 tablespoons sifted all-purpose
*   flour*
1½ cups milk, at room
*   temperature*

6 large egg yolks, at room
*   temperature*
½ cup lowfat ricotta cheese
1 teaspoon ground nutmeg,
*   preferably freshly grated*
Salt and freshly ground white
*   pepper to taste*

5. Lightly grease 2 shallow baking pans. Arrange half the eggplant slices in a single layer in both pans. Spread 2 tablespoons of the filling to the edges on top of each eggplant slice. Then top each with a slice of potato followed by a slice of feta. Using the remaining eggplant slices, top each moussaka with an eggplant slice.

6. To prepare the topping: In a heavy 2- to 3-quart saucepan over low heat, melt the butter. Whisk in the flour until large bubbles appear, about 3 minutes. Cook, whisking constantly, 2 minutes more; do not let the *roux* brown. Gradually add the milk, still whisking constantly over the bottom and side of the pan. Bring to a boil, and boil for 4 minutes, whisking until smooth and thickened. In a small bowl whisk ¼ cup of the hot mixture into the egg yolks, then whisk this mixture back into the pan. Bring to a second boil, whisking constantly, and boil for 3 minutes, whisking until smooth and thick enough to pipe. Whisk in the ricotta cheese and nutmeg, and season with salt and pepper. Let cool to room temperature. Transfer the topping to a pastry bag fitted with a medium star tip and pipe a large rosette on top of each moussaka.

7. Bake for 30 to 35 minutes or until the custard is set. Serve hot.

BOURBON-GLAZED SWEET POTATO AND BANANA PONE

(UNITED STATES)

Serves 4 to 6

3 medium-sized cooked sweet
  potatoes (page 133), peeled
  and cut in half lengthwise
3 large eggs
1 tablespoon unsulfured
  molasses
½ teaspoon ground allspice
½ teaspoon ground nutmeg,
  preferably freshly grated
¼ teaspoon ground ginger
3 ripe but firm bananas, cut in
  half crosswise, then halved
  lengthwise
⅓ cup dried currants or seedless
  raisins
¼ cup bourbon
2 tablespoons unsalted butter,
  melted

1. Preheat the oven to 275°F.

2. Arrange the cooked sweet potatoes in a single layer cut side down in a 2-quart round baking dish or gratin dish.

3. In a medium bowl whisk together the eggs, molasses, allspice, nutmeg and ginger until well blended. Pour this mixture over the potatoes in the baking dish.

4. Arrange the 12 banana slices over the potatoes in a pinwheel pattern, beginning at the center of the dish. Sprinkle evenly with the currants and drizzle with the bourbon. Lightly brush the bananas with the butter.

5. Bake for 40 to 50 minutes until the top is lightly browned. Serve hot directly from the baking dish, as a side dish to baked ham, roasted pork, or beef.

> *"The potato is one of nature's best-designed products; it is born in a sturdy package, with a wonderful shelf-life."*
> —*John and Karen Hess,* Viva *magazine, 1978*

1. To prepare the filling: In a large bowl combine the flour, salt, and pepper and mix until well blended. Dredge the lamb in the flour mixture until evenly coated, shaking off excess flour.

2. In a heavy 3- to 4-quart saucepan over medium-high heat, heat the oil. Add the lamb in batches and sear, turning often so cubes brown evenly on all sides, about 4 to 5 minutes per batch. Transfer the lamb to a medium bowl as it is browned and reserve.

3. Pour the stock into the saucepan (be careful—the liquid may splatter) and stir, scraping up the browned bits from the bottom and around the side of the saucepan. Stir in the reserved lamb, red wine, tomato paste, mushrooms, carrots, raisins, garlic, cumin, oregano, and marjoram and season with salt and pepper. Bring to a boil. Reduce the heat to low and simmer for 15 minutes, stirring occasionally. Stir in the peas until well blended.

Filling:

¼ cup all-purpose flour

¼ teaspoon salt

½ teaspoon freshly ground pepper

1 pound lean boneless lamb, preferably from the shoulder, trimmed and cut into 1-inch cubes

2 tablespoons safflower oil or olive oil

1 cup homemade beef stock or canned low-sodium beef broth

¾ cup dry red wine

2 tablespoons tomato paste, preferably Italian

14 ounces mushrooms, preferably short stem, wiped clean with a damp paper towel and thinly sliced

2 medium carrots or parsnips, cut into ⅛-inch-thick slices

½ cup seedless golden raisins or dried currants

3 cloves garlic, crushed

SHEPHERD'S PIE WITH ORANGE-POTATO TOPPING

(SCOTLAND)

Serves 4 to 6

1 teaspoon ground cumin

1 tablespoon finely chopped
  fresh oregano or 2 teaspoons
  dried, crumbled

2 teaspoons finely chopped fresh
  marjoram or 1 teaspoon dried,
  crumbled

Salt and freshly ground pepper
  to taste

½ cup fresh or thawed frozen
  green peas

Topping:

4 cups firmly packed smooth
  mashed potatoes (page 139),
  at room temperature

⅔ cup milk, plus more,
  depending on consistency
  needed to pipe

1 teaspoon freshly grated
  orange zest

¼ teaspoon salt

¼ teaspoon freshly ground
  white pepper

2 tablespoons milk, to glaze

4. Preheat the oven to 375°F.

5. Transfer the lamb mixture to a 9- by 9- by 2-inch baking dish, smoothing the top with a spatula. (The recipe can be made up to this point 1 day ahead. Let cool, wrap, and refrigerate. Bring to room temperature before proceeding.)

6. To prepare the topping: In a large bowl mix together the mashed potatoes, milk, orange zest, salt, and pepper until well blended. Transfer the topping to a pastry bag fitted with a large star tip. Pipe 5 straight, parallel lines of topping 1½ inches apart. Repeat, drawing lines over the first group to form a grid. Then pipe a large rosette of topping in every square to form a checkerboard pattern.

7. Lightly brush the surface of the topping with the 2 tablespoons milk. Bake for 45 to 50 minutes or until the top is golden brown. Let stand for 10 minutes before serving. Serve hot directly from the baking dish.

1 package (¼ ounce) active dry
   yeast
1 cup warm water (110°F.)
2 tablespoons sugar
2 medium-sized cooked baking
   potatoes (page 132), peeled
   and coarsely mashed (enough
   to make 1 firmly packed cup)
⅓ cup lowfat buttermilk
3 tablespoons unsalted butter, at
   room temperature
2 teaspoons salt
2 cloves garlic, crushed
¼ cup finely chopped fresh dill
½ teaspoon ground cayenne
   (red) pepper
6 cups sifted bread flour, plus
   more to dust work surface and
   knead dough
Olive oil, to grease bowl and
   loaf pan

1. In a small heatproof bowl whisk together the yeast with the water. Add the sugar and whisk together until the yeast is dissolved. Set aside for 10 minutes or until the surface is frothy. (*Note*: If bubbles do not appear within 10 minutes, discard mixture and repeat process.)

2. Meanwhile, in a large bowl mix together the mashed potatoes, buttermilk, butter, salt, garlic, dill, cayenne, and 5 cups of the bread flour until well blended. Stir in the yeast mixture and mix well until a soft, sticky dough forms.

3. Turn the dough onto a lightly floured surface; knead for 30 turns, adding the remaining flour until elastic.

4. Lightly grease a large bowl with olive oil. Transfer the dough to the bowl and turn once to coat lightly with the oil. Cover with a towel and let stand in a warm, draft-free place for 1½ hours or until doubled in size.

5. Lightly grease a 9- by 5- by 3-inch loaf pan.

6. Transfer the dough to a lightly floured work surface, and gently punch the dough down to deflate it. Knead it for 10 turns. Form the dough into a loaf and place it in the loaf pan, seam side down. Cover with a towel and let rise for 30 to 40 minutes or until it has risen 1 inch above the rim of the pan.

7. Preheat the oven to 350°F.

8. Using kitchen scissors or a sharp knife, slash the top of the loaf with three ¼-inch-deep parallel incisions. Bake the loaf for 50 to 60 minutes or until golden brown on top and the bread sounds hollow when tapped.

9. Allow the bread to cool in the pan. Then remove from the pan and finish cooling on a wire rack before slicing.

ILLED BUTTERMILK POTATO BREAD

(UNITED STATES)
Makes 1 9- by
5- by 3-inch loaf

55

Dough:

Olive oil, to grease bowl and
  pizza pan
2 medium-sized cooked baking
  potatoes (page 132), peeled
  and mashed (enough to make
  1 cup firmly packed smooth
  mashed potatoes)
2 cups sifted bread flour, plus
  more to dust work surface and
  knead dough
1 tablespoon finely chopped
  fresh sage or 1½ teaspoons
  ground dried sage
½ teaspoon salt
½ teaspoon freshly ground
  pepper
1 teaspoon active dry yeast
½ cup warm milk (110°F.)
½ teaspoon sugar

1. Lightly oil a 9-inch pizza pan.

2. To prepare the dough: In a large bowl combine the mashed potatoes, bread flour, sage, salt, and pepper. In a separate heatproof bowl whisk together the yeast with the milk. Add the sugar and whisk together until the yeast is dissolved. Set aside for about 10 minutes or until the surface is frothy. (*Note:* If bubbles do not appear within 10 minutes, discard mixture and repeat process.)

3. Stir the yeast mixture into the potato mixture and mix until a soft dough forms. Transfer the dough to a lightly floured work surface and knead about 20 turns, or until dough is smooth and elastic. Lightly grease a medium bowl with the olive oil. Transfer the dough to the bowl and turn the dough once to coat it with the oil. Cover with a towel and let stand in a warm, draft-free place about 1½ hours or until doubled in size.

4. Transfer the dough to a lightly floured work surface, gently punch dough down, and knead 2 turns more. Place the dough on the oiled pizza pan and using your fingers press

POTATO PIZZA WITH CARAMELIZED SHALLOTS

(ITALY)

Makes 1 9-inch pizza,
Serves 2,
3 slices per serving

the dough out so it spreads to the edge to form an even crust. Pinch the edge to form a 1-inch high rim.

5. To prepare the topping: In a heavy large skillet over medium heat, melt the butter. Add the shallots and cook, covered, stirring occasionally, for about 20 minutes.

6. Stir in the sugar, red wine vinegar, salt, and pepper and cook, stirring, for 5 to 8 minutes or until the shallots are a deep golden brown. (The shallot mixture can be prepared up to 1 day in advance. Let cool to room temperature, wrap, and refrigerate.)

7. Preheat the oven to 425°F.

8. Drain the shallot mixture and spread the mixture over the dough to the edge. Distribute the shredded mozzarella over the top, and sprinkle with the bacon. Bake for 15 to 20 minutes or until the cheese is melted and the dough is crisp and golden. Cut into 8 slices and place a whole basil leaf on each slice, the tip of the leaf pointing towards the center. Serve at once.

> *"Many battles were fought. But sometimes after a battle the general looked at his muddied uniform and bent sword, and thought of a baked potato and a soft bed."*
> —*Anita Lobel*, Potatoes, Potatoes, *1967*

Topping:
¼ cup (½ stick) unsalted butter
12 ounces shallots, very thinly sliced
1 tablespoon sugar
2 tablespoons red wine vinegar
½ teaspoon salt
½ teaspoon freshly ground pepper
6 ounces part skim-milk mozzarella, shredded
6 strips lean slab bacon, fried until crisp and crumbled, to garnish
8 whole fresh basil leaves, to garnish

 **HORIZO-POTATO QUESADILLAS**

(MEXICO)

Serves 4, 3 quesadillas

per serving

2 teaspoons safflower oil or
vegetable oil
1 medium yellow onion, coarsely
chopped
4 ounces fresh chorizo (Mexican
spicy pork-based sausage or
spicy Spanish smoked pork-
based sausage), very finely
chopped (available at butcher
shop or gourmet store)
2 medium-sized cooked boiling
potatoes (page 133), peeled
and cut into ¼-inch dice
(enough to make 3 cups)
2 large ripe tomatoes, peeled,
seeded, and finely chopped
1 to 2 fresh jalapeño peppers
(depending on desired
hotness), seeded, ribs removed,
and minced
½ teaspoon salt
½ teaspoon freshly ground
pepper
1½ tablespoons unsalted butter,
softened at room temperature,
plus more to grease
12 7-inch flour tortillas
4 ounces Monterey Jack cheese,
shredded

Sour cream or plain lowfat
yogurt, to serve
Guacamole (Mexican avocado-
based sauce), to serve
Salsa Picante (Mexican red
tomato sauce), to serve

1. In a large heavy skillet over medium-high heat, heat the oil. Add the onion and *chorizo* and cook, stirring often, for 15 to 20 minutes or until the onion is golden and *chorizo* is browned evenly. Carefully pour off the fat.

2. Add the potatoes, tomatoes, jalapeño, salt, and pepper, and cook, stirring often, for 5 to 8 minutes or until the mixture is somewhat dry. Remove from the heat and reserve. You should have 3 lightly packed cups filling.

3. Preheat the oven to 400°F. Lightly butter a baking sheet.

4. Lay the tortillas out on a work surface. Spread ¼ cup of the *chorizo* filling over half of each tortilla. Sprinkle the same half of each tortilla with the cheese. Fold the uncovered half of each tortilla over the filled half, gently pressing down on the filling to flatten and seal the tortilla closed, forming a half-moon.

5. Arrange the *quesadillas* on the buttered baking sheet about 1 inch apart. Lightly brush the surface of each with the butter and bake for 10 to 15 minutes or until toasted and the edges are golden brown. Serve hot, with dollops of sour cream and guacamole on each. Pass the salsa separately.

Note: To prepare fresh jalapeño peppers: The oil from jalapeños can act as an irritant, so wear rubber gloves when prepping the peppers, and always wash your hands well after handling. Before cutting the pepper, rinse and remove the stem under cold, running water. Slice the pepper in half lengthwise, and remove and discard the seeds. Using a sharp knife, remove and discard the white, fleshy ribs. The jalapeño pepper is ready to be used according to recipe instructions.

 WEET POTATO SILVER DOLLARS

(UNITED STATES)
*Serves 4, 8 2½-inch
pancakes per serving*

4 large eggs
½ teaspoon salt
*½ teaspoon double-acting
  baking powder*
¼ cup sifted cake flour
1 tablespoon sugar
*1 cup firmly packed mashed
  sweet potatoes (page 139),
  preferably variety labeled
  yams (page 133)*
*3 tablespoons unsalted butter,
  melted*
¼ cup milk
¼ teaspoon ground cinnamon
*⅛ teaspoon ground nutmeg,
  preferably freshly grated*
*1 teaspoon peeled freshly grated
  gingerroot*
*2 tablespoons safflower oil, to
  grease*

*Warm maple syrup or honey, to
  serve*
Butter, to serve

1. In a medium bowl beat together the eggs, salt, baking powder, flour, sugar, mashed sweet potatoes, melted butter, milk, cinnamon, nutmeg, and gingerroot until smooth.

2. Heat a medium nonstick skillet or griddle over medium heat until very hot. (To test: Run your hand under water, and flick water onto the skillet. It is ready when the water drops bead and dance.) Coat skillet lightly with the safflower oil.

3. Drop tablespoonfuls of batter into the skillet, making sure that when they spread out they measure less than 3 inches in diameter. Cook 3 or 4 minutes, or until a few bubbles appear on the surface of the pancakes, then flip over and cook the other side about 1 minute. Repeat with the remaining batter, adding more oil if needed to coat the skillet in between batches. Keep the pancakes in a very low oven to keep warm until ready to serve. Serve with warm maple syrup (or honey) and butter for guests to help themselves.

> *"There is no species of human food that can be consumed in a greater variety of modes than the potato."*
> *—Sir John Sinclair, 1828*

MALARABIA

(Guava, Plantain, and Sweet Potato Compote)

1½ cups guava nectar or juice
   blend (available at health
   food store or supermarket)
¼ cup fresh lemon juice
3 medium-sized cooked sweet
   potatoes (page 136), preferably
   variety labeled yams (page
   133), peeled and cut into ½-
   inch dice
2 large ripe but firm plantains
2 tablespoons firmly packed
   light brown sugar
2 tablespoons dark rum
½ teaspoon ground cinnamon
¼ teaspoon ground cloves
¼ teaspoon ground nutmeg,
   preferably freshly grated
¼ teaspoon ground allspice
½ cup canned cream of coconut
   (available at supermarket)

1. In a nonreactive heavy 4- to 5-quart saucepan over medium heat, combine the guava juice, lemon juice, and sweet potatoes and bring to a boil.

2. Meanwhile, peel the plantains. Trim the ends of the fruit and cut the plantains in half lengthwise. Remove and discard the fiber that runs down the center of the fruit. Cut the plantains crosswise into ¼-inch-thick slices.

3. Raise the heat to medium-high. Stir the plantains, ½ cup water, the brown sugar, rum, cinnamon, cloves, nutmeg, and allspice into the saucepan until well blended. Bring the mixture to a boil. Then reduce heat to low and simmer for 15 to 20 minutes more, stirring often, or until the plantains begin to fall apart and the mixture has thickened.

4. Remove the saucepan from the heat, and transfer the mixture to a medium heatproof bowl. Stir ¼ cup of the hot mixture into the cream of coconut in a small bowl, then stir this mixture back into the medium bowl until well blended. Let cool to room temperature before serving. (The recipe can be made up to this point 3 days ahead. Let cool, wrap, and refrigerate. Bring to room temperature before serving.) Serve with a pork, chicken, or beef entrée.

(PUERTO RICO)

Makes about 5½ cups

Bread:

1 large baking potato, washed thoroughly and peeled

Safflower oil or vegetable oil, to grease

1½ cups sifted all-purpose flour

1 tablespoon double-acting baking powder

⅔ cup sugar

½ cup unsweetened cocoa powder

½ teaspoon salt

¼ teaspoon freshly ground pepper

1 large egg

½ cup (1 stick) unsalted butter, melted

Confectioners' sugar, to garnish (optional)

Orange-Chocolate Butter:

Makes about ½ cup

½ cup (1 stick) unsalted butter, at room temperature

1 tablespoon freshly grated orange zest

1 ounce semisweet chocolate, finely chopped

Raspberry preserves, to serve (optional)

1. To prepare the bread: Place the potato directly on a rack or in a steamer basket in a 3-quart saucepan over 2 inches of boiling water (the water level should not touch the bottom of the rack). Cover the saucepan and steam the potato for 25 to 30 minutes or until it tests done. Drain, reserving 1½ cups of the cooking water. Using a potato masher or potato ricer, mash the potato until smooth. You will need 1 cup firmly packed mashed potato. Reserve the cooking liquid and mashed potato separately.

2. Preheat the oven to 350°F. Lightly grease the loaf pans.

3. Sift together the flour, baking powder, sugar, cocoa powder, salt, and pepper into a large bowl.

4. In a medium bowl beat together the egg, melted butter, the reserved 1 cup mashed potato, and the reserved 1½ cups potato cooking liquid just until combined. Pour the liquid mixture into the flour mixture, and stir just until blended, being careful not to overmix.

★ SPUD SUPERSTITIONS OR LUMPER LORE ★

For a bountiful yield, the potato should be planted in the dark of the moon.

Italian "voodoo": Write the name of your victim on a piece of paper and using as many pins as possible tack the paper to a potato. The person will die a painful death within a month.

A potato flower (even though it is poisonous) means benevolence for its owner.

5. Fill each miniature loaf pan two-thirds full, or fill the large loaf pan. Using a knife, smooth the top of each.

6. Bake the miniature loaves for 30 to 35 minutes, the large loaf for 45 to 50 minutes or until it tests done when it is pierced in the center with a cake tester or toothpick and it comes out clean. Let stand for 10 minutes before serving. (The recipe can be made up to this point 2 days ahead. Let cool completely in pans. Remove from pans, wrap, and refrigerate. Bring to room temperature before serving.)

7. Meanwhile, prepare the butter: In a small bowl beat the butter until soft. Stir in the orange zest and chocolate until well blended.

8. To serve, carefully remove the bread from the pans. Using a fine-mesh sieve, lightly dust the top of the bread with the confectioners' sugar, if desired. Serve warm or at room temperature. Pass with the orange-chocolate butter or the raspberry preserves if desired.

POTATO-CHOCOLATE BREAD WITH ORANGE-CHOCOLATE BUTTER

(UNITED STATES)

Makes 6 4- by 2- by 1½-inch
miniature loaves or 1
9- by 5- by 3-inch loaf

SWEET POTATO CUSTARD

Safflower oil or vegetable oil, to
    grease
⅓ cup firmly packed mashed
    sweet potatoes (page 139)
½ cup sugar
½ cup half-and-half
½ cup skim milk
2 large eggs
1 large egg yolk
½ teaspoon ground cinnamon
¼ teaspoon ground cloves
¼ teaspoon ground ginger
¼ teaspoon ground nutmeg,
    preferably freshly grated
¼ teaspoon salt
¼ teaspoon freshly ground
    pepper
¼ cup seedless golden raisins or
    dried currants, soaked for 15
    minutes in the rum, drained,
    and rum discarded
4 cups boiling water

Rum-spiked fresh whipped
    cream, to serve (optional)

> *"Never eat more than
> you can lift."*
>
> *—Miss Piggy*

(CARIBBEAN)
Serves 4

1. Preheat the oven to 350°F. Liberally grease 4 heatproof custard cups (⅔-cup capacity) and arrange in a 13- by 9- by 2-inch baking pan.

2. In a medium bowl beat together the mashed sweet potatoes, sugar, half-and-half, skim milk, eggs, egg yolk, cinnamon, cloves, ginger, nutmeg, salt, and pepper until smooth. Stir in the drained raisins, until well blended. Divide the mixture evenly among the custard cups.

3. Carefully pour the boiling water into the corner of the baking pan, around the custard cups to the depth of 1 inch. Using potholders (the pan will be hot), transfer the pan to the middle rack of the oven and bake for 45 to 50 minutes or until a knife inserted near the center comes out clean.

4. Remove the cups from the pan and let cool to room temperature. Wrap and refrigerate the custards for at least 2 hours or until thoroughly chilled. (The recipe can be prepared up to this point 1 day ahead.)

5. To serve, run a knife around the inside of each custard cup to release the custard from the edge. Dip the bottom of the cup briefly in hot water, then wipe the outside of the cup dry. Invert onto a chilled dessert plate or serve directly from the cups. Serve with rum-spiked whipped cream if desired.

DOWN-UNDER ROADSIDE PASTIES

(AUSTRALIA)

*Makes 20
3-inch pasties*

Pastry:

*3 cups sifted all-purpose flour,
    plus more to dust*

1 teaspoon salt

*½ cup (1 stick) unsalted
    margarine, diced and chilled*

*¼ cup safflower oil or vegetable
    oil, plus more to grease*

Filling:

*½ pound trimmed flank steak,
    very finely chopped*

*1 medium yellow onion, very
    finely chopped*

*1 small turnip, peeled and
    grated*

*1 medium-sized cooked boiling
    potato (page 136), peeled and
    cut into ¼-inch dice*

2 teaspoons fennel seed, crushed

*Salt and freshly ground pepper
    to taste*

3 tablespoons milk, to glaze

*Australian tomato sauce
    (ketchup), to serve*

1. To prepare the pastry: In a medium bowl sift together the flour and salt. Using a pastry blender or fork, cut in the margarine until the mixture resembles coarse crumbs. Stir in the safflower oil and ¼ cup water until a well blended and smooth, soft dough forms. Form into a flat disk and wrap in waxed paper. Refrigerate until ready to use.

2. Meanwhile, prepare the filling: In a medium bowl stir together the steak, onion, and turnip until well blended. Stir in the potato and fennel seed and season with salt and pepper, stirring gently until well blended. You should have about 3 tightly packed cups of filling.

3. On a lightly floured work surface, using a well-floured rolling pin, roll the dough out to a uniform ⅛-inch thickness. Using a floured 3-inch biscuit cutter, cut the dough into 3-inch rounds, dipping the cutter back into the flour in between cuts. Reroll the scraps of dough and repeat until you have 40 rounds.

4. Preheat the oven to 400°F. Lightly oil a baking sheet with safflower oil.

5. Place a dough round on the prepared baking sheet and place 1 heaping tablespoon of filling in the center of the round. Using your fingers, lightly moisten the edge of the round with water, and place a second round on top. Using a fork, press the edges to crimp and seal them together. With a round or shaped aspic cutter punch out a hole in the top of the round to expose the filling or prick twice with a fork to allow steam to escape. Repeat with the remaining rounds and filling, placing the pasties ½ inch apart on the baking sheet. Lightly brush the surface of each pasty with milk.

6. Bake for 30 to 35 minutes or until crisp and the edges are golden brown. Serve hot, and pass with ketchup for guests to help themselves.

★ SPUD-TACULAR EXTRAVAGANZA ★

There is so much experimentation with new crops that it is next to impossible to get an accurate count of the types of potatoes now being grown. One source said that there are 400 varieties but less than 30 types are being cultivated. Another source said there are 10,000 types in existence, but I suppose all that matters is how many types reach your store! Some of the ancient potato varieties are being rediscovered. I call them "heritage" potatoes. The names alone are better than Crayon color names. Here is a sample: Pink Fir, French La Ratte, Siberian, Lady Fingers, Peanut, Tobique, Warba (Pink Eye), Viking Purple, Sangre, Huckleberry, Alaska Sweetheart, Caribe, Bison, Sunrise, Pink Pearl, Purple Peruvian, All Blue, Candy Stripe, Larota . . . I suspect that your store could at any given time supply you with as many as 15 types (some will be early crops, others will be main crops). This is a good springboard for the culinary realization of the potato's true potential. You won't be able to find all in your local market, but the potato is a bestseller, and its popularity is growing day by day. Smart shopkeepers are always expanding their range of varieties, so, if they don't have a particular type you want, just ask!

¾ cup firmly packed smooth
    mashed potatoes (page 139)
5 large eggs, separated
3 ounces pecans, very finely
    ground in a food processor
    fitted with a metal blade
    (enough to make 1 cup finely
    ground)
¼ cup flavorful light-colored
    honey
½ cup sugar
Safflower oil or unsalted butter,
    to grease

Unsweetened whipped cream, to
    serve (optional)
Fresh ripe blackberries,
    raspberries, blueberries, or
    strawberries, or a combination
    of fresh ripe Bing or Royal
    Ann cherries, to serve
    (optional)

1. In a large bowl stir together the mashed potatoes, egg yolks, ground pecans, and honey until well blended.

2. Preheat the oven to 325°F. Lightly grease the bottom of an 8-inch cake pan and line with waxed or parchment paper. Lightly grease the top of the paper and side of the pan.

3. In another medium bowl combine the sugar and egg whites and beat until they form stiff peaks. Working quickly, stir about ¼ cup of the egg white mixture into the potato mixture, then fold the remaining egg whites into the potato mixture until well blended.

4. Pour the mixture into the prepared pan, smoothing the top. Place the pan on the middle rack of the oven and bake for 45 to 55 minutes or until a toothpick inserted in the center comes out clean.

5. Let the torte cool in the cake pan for 15 minutes. Then carefully run a knife around the edges to release the torte from the pan. Using two thin spatulas or your hands, very carefully lift the torte straight out onto a cake rack. (Do not invert torte to avoid marks from the rack on top of the torte.) Remove and discard the waxed paper from the bottom of the torte. Let finish cooling to room temperature.

6. To serve, cut into wedges and serve at room temperature. Decorate each slice with a dollop of whipped cream and fresh berries if desired. To store: Let cool completely, wrap tightly, and keep in an airtight tin at room temperature for up to 2 days.

(UNITED STATES)

*Makes 1 8-inch torte,
serving 4 to 6*

FLOURLESS HONEY-PECAN POTATO TORTE

POTATO-CHEESE STRUDEL WITH CANDIED FRUIT

(GERMANY)

Serves 4 to 6

Filling:

¼ *cup lowfat cottage cheese*

¼ *cup sour cream or plain lowfat yogurt*

½ *cup smooth firmly packed mashed potatoes (page 139)*

2 tablespoons sugar

1 large egg, lightly beaten

1½ teaspoons freshly grated lemon zest

1 teaspoon pure vanilla extract

½ *cup finely chopped assorted candied or dried fruit*

Safflower oil or vegetable oil, to grease

Pastry:

Four 12-by-17-inch sheets of phyllo (available at supermarket), stacked between 2 sheets of waxed paper and covered with damp paper towels

2 tablespoons unsalted butter, melted

½ *cup unseasoned dry bread crumbs*

Confectioners' sugar, to garnish (optional)

1. To prepare the filling: In a medium bowl mix together the cottage cheese, sour cream, mashed potatoes, sugar, and egg just until well blended; do not overmix. Stir in the lemon zest, vanilla, and candied fruit until blended.

2. Preheat the oven to 350°F. Line a baking sheet with parchment paper or lightly grease.

3. To assemble the pastry: Place a kitchen towel with long side facing you on a work surface, cover it with 1 phyllo sheet, and brush the sheet with a little of the butter. Working quickly, repeat the process with the remaining sheets of phyllo, layering them using a total of only 1 tablespoon of the melted butter. Sprinkle the phyllo evenly with the bread crumbs, leaving a 2-inch margin on all sides.

4. Spoon the cheese mixture on the bread crumbs along the long side of the dough, leaving the 2-inch margin uncovered. Working quickly, using the towel as a guide, roll up the strudel tightly lengthwise, enclosing the filling. Carefully transfer the strudel seam-side-down to the prepared baking sheet. Trim the ends on bias and discard the ends. Using a bread knife cut the strudel very lightly on the bias to score 8 equal portions, but do not cut through the crust. Brush the entire surface of the strudel with the remaining 1 tablespoon melted butter.

5. Bake in the middle rack of the oven for 30 to 40 minutes or until crisp and lightly browned.

6. To serve, let stand for 10 minutes, then finish cutting through the strudel. Using a fine-mesh sieve lightly dust the top of each strudel portion through a decorative pastry stencil (available at a gourmet or baking shop) with confectioners' sugar if desired. Serve hot or at room temperature.

Crust:

Makes enough pastry for 1 single 8- or 9-inch pie crust

1½ cups sifted all-purpose flour, plus more to dust

½ teaspoon salt

¼ cup vegetable shortening

½ cup firmly packed smooth mashed sweet potato (page 139), preferably variety labeled yams (page 135)

3 to 4 tablespoons ice water

1. To prepare the crust: In a medium bowl sift together the flour and salt. Using a pastry blender or fork, cut in the vegetable shortening and mashed sweet potato until the mixture resembles coarse cornmeal. Then stir in the ice water, a tablespoon at a time, as needed to allow dough to form but not become sticky. Form into a flat disk. Wrap in waxed paper and chill at least 30 minutes until ready to use. (The dough can be prepared ahead, wrapped, and refrigerated up to 1 day. Bring to room temperature before proceeding with recipe.)

2. To prepare the filling: In the top of a double boiler over barely simmering water, combine the chocolate and butter and melt. Transfer to a small heatproof bowl and let cool to room temperature.

3. Preheat the oven to 400°F.

4. Meanwhile, on a lightly floured work surface, using a lightly floured rolling pin, roll out the dough ⅛ inch thick. Trim to fit the bottom of an 8- or 9-inch pie plate with a 1-inch overhang. Very lightly moisten the edge of the pie plate with water and line with the crust (avoid stretching the crust or it will shrink when baked). Fold under the extra pastry to build up the rim and crimp to form a pretty edge. Reroll the scraps of dough and, using a cookie cutter of your

CHOCOLATE PECAN PIE WITH SWEET POTATO CRUST

choice up to 3½ inches in diameter, cut out 8 shapes to garnish the top of the pie. Transfer the decorations to a waxed paper-lined baking sheet and refrigerate until ready to use.

5. In a large bowl beat the eggs until light and fluffy. Beat in the sugar, corn syrup, maple syrup, vanilla, and salt until well blended. Beat in the cooled chocolate mixture. Stir in the pecans until well blended.

6. Pour the filling into the pie crust. Decorate the surface of the filling with reserved crust shapes, and sprinkle each with a little of the sugar if desired. Transfer the pie to a baking sheet. Bake on the middle rack of the oven for 15 minutes. Reduce the heat to 350°F. and bake for 30 to 40 minutes more, or until the center of the filling is almost set. (*Note*: The very center of the pie should be slightly soft, while the edge and near center will be set.) Be careful not to overbake. The filling will fully set as it cools.

7. To serve, let the pie stand for 15 minutes before cutting. Serve warm or at room temperature. Slice, and serve with dollops of whipped cream garnished with chocolate curls if desired. To store: Let cool to room temperature, wrap tightly, and refrigerate for up to 2 days. Return to room temperature before serving.

(UNITED STATES)

Makes 1 8- or 9-inch pie,

serving 6 to 8

Filling:

3 ounces unsweetened chocolate, finely chopped

¼ cup (½ stick) unsalted butter

3 large eggs, at room temperature

¾ cup sugar

¾ cup dark corn syrup

½ cup maple syrup

1½ teaspoons pure vanilla extract

¼ teaspoon salt

5 ounces whole pecan halves

⅛ teaspoon sugar, to garnish (optional)

Unsweetened whipped cream flavored with ⅛ teaspoon ground ginger, to serve (optional)

Chocolate curls, to garnish (optional)

Mashed, Scalloped, and Au Gratin

3

HINESE-STYLE MASHED POTATOES

(CHINA)

Serves 4

*2 cups firmly packed mashed
potatoes (page 139) from
baked potatoes below*

*3 tablespoons "lite" soy sauce
(available at supermarket)*

*2 tablespoons black sesame
seeds (available at Oriental
market) or white sesame
seeds, toasted in preheated
350°F. oven for 2 or 3 minutes,
stirring often*

*1 tablespoon pure Oriental
sesame oil (available at
Oriental market)*

Freshly ground pepper to taste

*4 medium-sized baked potato
skin shells (from scooped-out
baked baking potatoes)*

*Safflower oil or vegetable oil, to
grease*

*3 ounces chow mein noodles
(deep-fried Chinese noodles,
available at supermarket or
Oriental market)*

1. Preheat the oven to 350°F.

2. In a medium bowl combine the mashed potatoes, soy sauce, sesame seeds, and sesame oil. Season with pepper. Firmly pack one quarter of the mashed potato mixture into each potato shell. Repeat until you have 4 filled potato shells. Transfer to a lightly greased baking sheet. Using a quarter of the chow mein noodles, "stud" the top of each stuffed potato to resemble a porcupine. Bake for 10 to 15 minutes or until heated through.

3. Serve hot as an appetizer or as a side dish to a beef or pork main course.

> *"There are many ways to love a vegetable. The most sensible way is to love it well-treated. Then you can eat it with the comfortable knowledge that you will be a better man for it, in your spirit and your body too . . ."*
> —*M.F.K. Fisher,* How To Cook A Wolf, *1951*

Life to you is a dashing and bold
adventure. ☺

SWISS-STYLE MASHED POTATOES

*Safflower oil or vegetable oil, to
 grease*

*3 cups firmly packed mashed
 potatoes (page 139)*

1 tablespoon red currant jelly

*1 teaspoon freshly ground white
 pepper*

*2 tablespoons unsalted butter,
 melted*

¼ teaspoon ground cinnamon

⅛ teaspoon ground cloves

*1 16-ounce can pear halves,
 packed in extra-light syrup,
 strained, juice reserved, and
 each pear half cut in half
 lengthwise*

> *"What I say is, that
> if a man really likes
> potatoes, he must be
> a pretty decent sort of
> fellow."*
> —*A.A. Milne*, Not
> That It Matters

(SWITZERLAND)

Serves 4

1. Preheat the oven to 350°F. Lightly grease the inside of 4 (¾-cup) timbale molds or custard cups.

2. In a medium bowl combine the mashed potatoes, currant jelly, pepper, melted butter, cinnamon, and cloves until well blended. Using ¾ cup of the mixture at a time, pack down into each prepared mold.

3. Invert each mold onto a lightly greased baking sheet, and shake gently to help the mashed potato form loosen from the mold. Press 3 pear slices (uniform in size) cut side down into and around the sides of each mashed potato form in a vertical pattern, the tips of the pears meeting at the top. Repeat until you have 4 pear "pyramids."

4. Drizzle half of the reserved pear juice, reserving the remaining half, over the pears and transfer the baking sheet to the oven. Bake for 15 to 20 minutes or until the pears and mashed potatoes are heated through.

5. To serve, drizzle the remaining pear juice over the molds and serve at once. These potato molds make a nice accompaniment to a chicken, seafood, or pork entrée.

12 ounces marinated artichoke
   hearts, drained and cut
   lengthwise into eighths
   (available at supermarket or
   gourmet store)
4 cups cooked wild rice
Salt and freshly ground pepper
   to taste
2 medium-sized boiling
   potatoes, washed thoroughly,
   peeled, and sliced crosswise
   into ⅛-inch-thick slices,
   preferably using a food
   processor fitted with a slicing
   disk or a mandoline *following
   manufacturer's instructions*
1 cup homemade chicken stock
   or canned low-sodium chicken
   broth
¼ cup dry vermouth or dry
   white wine
4 medium-sized ripe but firm
   red or yellow tomatoes or a
   combination of both, very
   thinly sliced
¼ cup unseasoned dry bread
   crumbs
¼ cup freshly grated Parmesan
   cheese
3 tablespoons olive oil, plus more
   to grease

(FRANCE)

Serves 4 to 6

POTATO, TOMATO, AND ARTICHOKE GRATIN ON BED OF WILD RICE

1. Preheat the oven to 425°F. Lightly grease a 2-quart gratin dish or baking dish.

2. In a medium bowl combine the artichoke hearts and cooked wild rice until well blended. Season lightly with salt and pepper. Transfer the artichoke mixture to the bottom of the prepared gratin dish, smoothing evenly. Overlap the potato slices on top of the artichoke mixture in a pattern of parallel lines, but in a single layer. Season liberally with salt and pepper.

3. Pour the chicken stock, then the vermouth over the potatoes. Repeat the pattern of the potatoes with the tomatoes. If using both red and yellow, arrange the colors in alternating lines.

4. In a small bowl mix together the bread crumbs and Parmesan cheese until blended. Sprinkle evenly over the gratin. Drizzle the 3 tablespoons olive oil over all.

5. Bake for 10 minutes. Reduce the heat to 375°F. and bake for 40 to 50 minutes more or until the top is golden brown and crusty and almost all the liquid is gone. Serve hot directly from the dish. The gratin makes a wonderful vegetarian entrée or side dish to a chicken or fish main course.

1 tablespoon olive oil

*1 medium yellow onion, finely
chopped*

3 cloves garlic, finely chopped

3 medium carrots, shredded

*2½ cups firmly packed mashed
potatoes (page 139)*

*1½ tablespoons paprika,
preferably Hungarian sweet
paprika (Source Lists,
page 142)*

*8 strips lean slab bacon, fried
until crisp and crumbled*

½ teaspoon salt

*½ teaspoon freshly ground
pepper*

*3 cups tomato sauce, preferably
homemade*

*2 medium heads green cabbage
(a total of 3½ to 4 pounds),
tough outer leaves removed
and discarded, remaining
leaves separated and blanched
until tender and kept
immersed in cold water until
ready to use*

1. In a large heavy skillet over medium-high heat, heat the oil. Add the onion, garlic, and shredded carrots. Cook, stirring often, for 5 to 7 minutes or until soft but not browned. Drain and reserve.

2. In a medium bowl combine the carrot mixture with the potatoes, paprika, bacon, salt, and pepper and mix until well blended to make about 4 firmly packed cups of stuffing.

3. Preheat the oven to 350°F. Pour 1½ cups of the tomato sauce into the bottom of a 3- to 4-quart ovenproof casserole with a tight-fitting lid (the cabbage bundles should be placed in a single layer), preferably an unglazed clay cooker.

4. Drain the blanched cabbage leaves from the soaking water and choose the 12 largest leaves with the least tears, reserving the remaining leaves for another use. Place the leaves inner (hollow) side down next to each other on a work surface. Using a small sharp knife, slice off the raised part of the vein, as close as possible to the leaf. Then cut off the tip of the stem and discard. Repeat with the remaining leaves, then flip each leaf over, deveined side down.

5. Place a firmly packed ⅓ cup filling in the shape of a 2½-inch long log 1 inch above the stem end of the leaf. Fold the stem end of the leaf over the filling. Then fold the two sides of the leaf inward and over the stuffing. Roll the leaf up tightly to enclose the filling. Place the cabbage bundle seam side down into the casserole with the tomato sauce. Repeat with the remaining 11 blanched cabbage leaves and filling, arranging them in a single layer in the casserole.

6. Ladle the remaining tomato sauce over the bundles until evenly coated. (The recipe can be prepared up to this point 2 days ahead. Cover and refrigerate. Bring to room temperature before proceeding with the recipe.) Bake, covered, for 30 to 40 minutes or until heated through. Serve hot.

POTATO AND BACON-STUFFED CABBAGE BUNDLES

(POLAND)

Serves 4
3 bundles per serving

IRANIAN-STYLE CINNAMON SCALLOPED POTATOES WITH GRATED TURNIP

★ POTATO PARAPHERNALIA ★

Potato nails (aluminum kitchen nails inserted into a baking potato length-wise while it bakes, to promote an evenly baked potato)

Potato "eye" remover

Potato ricer

Potato scoop

Potato masher

Potato fork

Pommes Anna pan
(French copper pan made specifically for the dish *pommes Anna*, which was named for the French woman Anna Deslions and consists of overlapping potato slices resembling a flat cake)

---

2 tablespoons unsalted butter, melted

1 cup milk, at room temperature

1 teaspoon ground cinnamon

2 cups firmly packed shredded turnip (about 3 medium turnips)

Salt and freshly ground pepper to taste

4 medium-sized baking potatoes, washed thoroughly, peeled, and sliced lengthwise into ¹/₁₆-inch-thick slices, preferably using a food processor fitted with a slicing disk or a mandoline *following manufacturer's directions*

1. Preheat the oven to 400°F. Lightly grease a 2-quart gratin dish or baking dish with a little of the melted butter.

2. In a medium bowl whisk together the milk and cinnamon until well blended.

3. Place the grated turnip in a small bowl and season liberally with salt and pepper, tossing until well blended. Spread the turnip mixture in the bottom of the prepared gratin dish in a smooth even layer. Overlap the potato slices on top of the turnip mixture in a pattern of concentric circles and pour the milk mixture over all. Drizzle the remaining melted butter evenly over the top.

4. Bake for 20 minutes. Reduce the heat to 350°F. and bake for 50 to 60 minutes more or until the potato-turnip mixture has absorbed most of the liquid and the top is golden brown and crisp. Serve hot directly from the dish to accompany a pork, fish, or chicken entrée.

(IRAN)

Serves 4 to 6

ASHED POTATO–THYME SOUP WITH POPPED-CORN CROUTONS

(FRANCE)

Makes 4 ¾-cup
servings

2 tablespoons unsalted butter

1 medium yellow onion, minced

2 scallions, white part only,
thinly sliced

3 shallots, minced

2½ cups homemade chicken
stock or canned low-sodium
chicken broth

2 teaspoons finely chopped fresh
thyme or fresh tarragon

2 cups firmly packed smooth
mashed potatoes (page 139)

¼ cup dry white wine

Salt and freshly ground white
pepper to taste

1 cup popped popcorn, to garnish

3 tablespoons finely chopped
fresh chives, to garnish

1. In a heavy 2- to 3-quart saucepan over medium-high heat, melt the butter. Add the onion, scallions, and shallots and cook, stirring, about 3 or 4 minutes or until soft but not browned. Stir in the stock and thyme and bring to a boil, stirring occasionally.

2. Gradually stir in the potatoes in 1-cup increments. Bring to a second boil. Reduce the heat to low, stir in the wine, and simmer, for 5 minutes, stirring once or twice. Season with salt and pepper. Divide the soup among 4 shallow soup bowls and garnish each with ¼ cup popcorn and some of the chives. Serve at once.

"Potato: bland, amiable, and homely, an honest vegetable, giving honour where honour is due—in an honest soup."
—Della Lutes, The Country Kitchen, 1938

Dough:

2 cups firmly packed smooth
   mashed potatoes (page 139)
2 large eggs, lightly beaten
2 tablespoons unsalted butter,
   melted, plus more to grease
3 tablespoons minced onion
1½ cups sifted all-purpose flour,
   plus more to dust
½ teaspoon salt
¼ teaspoon freshly ground
   white pepper

Filling:

2 tablespoons safflower oil or
   vegetable oil
1 medium yellow onion, finely
   chopped
8 ounces mushrooms, wiped
   clean with a damp paper
   towel and finely chopped
1 teaspoon finely chopped fresh
   thyme or ½ teaspoon dried,
   crumbled
½ teaspoon salt
½ teaspoon freshly ground
   pepper
1 cup cooked medium-sized-
   grain kasha (roasted
   buckwheat groats)
¼ cup finely chopped fresh
   parsley
1 large egg yolk, lightly beaten
Sour cream or plain lowfat
   yogurt, to serve (optional)

POTATO-KASHA KNISHES

(SOVIET UNION)

Makes 2 dozen 2-inch knishes

1. To prepare the dough: In a medium bowl combine the mashed potatoes, eggs, melted butter, and onion. Stir in the flour, salt, and pepper and gently mix until well blended and a smooth dough forms.

2. On a well-floured work surface, using a well-floured rolling pin, roll the dough out to a uniform ¼-inch thickness. Cut the dough into 3-inch rounds, using a floured 3-inch biscuit cutter, dipping the cutter back into the flour between cuts. Reroll the scraps of dough and repeat the process until you have 24 rounds. Reserve at room temperature until ready to use.

4. Meanwhile, prepare the filling: In a large heavy skillet over medium-high heat, heat the oil. Add the onion, mushrooms, thyme, salt, and pepper. Cook, stirring often, for 5 to 8 minutes or until the mushrooms release their liquid and begin to brown. Remove the skillet from the heat and stir in the cooked kasha and parsley until well blended. You should have about 2 lightly packed cups filling.

5. Preheat the oven to 350°F. Lightly butter a baking sheet.

6. Place a dough round on the buttered baking sheet and place 2 heaping teaspoons of filling in the center of the round and draw the edges together over it, while pushing in the filling. Pinch firmly to seal to form a ball. Flip the knish over seam side down. Repeat the process with the remaining rounds and filling, placing the knishes ½ inch apart on the baking sheet. Lightly brush the surface of each knish with the beaten egg yolk and bake for 40 to 45 minutes or until crisp and the top is golden brown. Serve at once, and pass with sour cream if desired.

To Prepare Kasha

Makes 1 cup
1 large egg, lightly beaten
⅓ cup medium-granulation
*   kasha*
½ cup boiling water

In a small bowl combine the egg and kasha and stir until the grains are well coated. Place the kasha in a heavy medium skillet over high heat. Using a wooden spoon, stir the kasha vigorously for 3 to 4 minutes or until the egg has dried and the grains separate. Remove the skillet from the heat and add the boiling water all at once (be careful—the liquid may splatter), stirring until well blended. Reserve at room temperature until ready to use.

★ A POTATO HANGOVER? ★

Here are a few facts on intriguing potato-based alcoholic beverages:

Aquavit is a flavored Scandinavian liquor. The traditional beverage of choice for the *skal* (toast) at a smorgasbord is *aquavit*, "the water of life." It is distilled from fermented potato or grain mash and usually contains a 42 to 45 percent alcohol content by volume. Some of the many flavorings include: caraway or cuminseed, lemon or orange peel, cardamom, aniseed, and fennel. By the way, doing shots of *aquavit* has been likened to swallowing a flaming sword . . . so think twice before trying it!

Irish Poteen is a potato-based liquor. Due to its very high alcohol content, and the fact that distilling potatoes is prohibited in Ireland, the beverage is illegal.

Chicha, A Peruvian beer, is made with potatoes.

F.Y.I.:

★ Both Russian vodka and schnapps have been made with potatoes.

★ It has been said that wines made with a potato base have the potential, with some careful aging, to be as "smooth" as fine brandy.

HAKER-STYLE STEWED POTATOES

3 medium-sized cooked boiling
   potatoes (page 136), peeled
   and cut into ½-inch-thick
   slices
1 cup milk
2 tablespoons unsalted butter, at
   room temperature
Salt and freshly ground pepper
   to taste

In a heavy 3-quart saucepan over medium-low heat, combine the potatoes and milk, and bring to a boil. Boil gently for 20 to 25 minutes, stirring occasionally, or until the mixture has thickened and the potatoes have absorbed all the milk. (*Note:* Stir gently so as not to break the potatoes.) Stir in the butter until well blended and season with salt and pepper. Serve at once, as an accompaniment to a poultry, fish, or beef main course.

POTATO GAMES

★ "SPUD" Any number of people can play this dodge ball game, which keeps score by "spuds," or points against a person.

★ "COUNTING RHYME," which decides who is to be team captain before the start of a game. One player stands in the middle of a circle made by the other players. Each player clenches his fists, holding them out in front of him. The player in the center begins the selection by gently tapping his own fists together, then to the other players' fists in the circle (to the beat of the following rhyme). When a person's fists are tapped while the word "more" is said he is out of the circle. (Even if the counter is out, he can still continue counting.) The count continues until there is only one person left in the circle. That person becomes the team captain.

Rhyming Jingle: *ONE* potato, *TWO* potato, *THREE* potato, *FOUR. FIVE* potato, *SIX* potato, *SEVEN* potato, *MORE!*

KORDALIA

(Garlic Sauce or Dip)

(GREECE)

Makes about 3¼ cups

2 medium heads garlic, peeled
2 cups firmly packed smooth
  mashed potatoes (page 139)
1 cup olive oil
⅔ cup white wine vinegar
½ teaspoon salt
¾ cup Greek Kalamata olives or
  other brine-cured olives,
  rinsed, pitted, and halved
  lengthwise, to garnish
  (optional)

In the bowl of a food processor fitted with a metal blade, or in a blender, process the garlic until minced. Add the potatoes, ½ cup of the olive oil, vinegar, and salt, and process just until blended. With the machine running, through the feed tube gradually pour in the remaining olive oil in a slow, steady stream and process until incorporated and the sauce is completely smooth. (*Note*: This sauce should have a mayonnaise-like consistency.)

(The recipe can be made up to this point 1 day ahead. Wrap and refrigerate. Whisk and adjust seasoning to taste before serving.) Serve at room temperature or chilled, and garnish with the olives if desired. *Skordalia* can be used as a sauce for seafood, meat, or vegetables or it can be served as a dip accompanied by raw vegetables (*crudités*) and hot pita bread (Middle Eastern pocket bread).

★ OTHER INTERNATIONAL MASHED POTATO DISHES ★

★ Chilean-Style: Combine cooked pumpkin, fried rice, and mashed potatoes.

★ French-Style: Combine slices of *foie gras* (French goose liver) and mashed potatoes.

★ Brazilian-Style: Combine cooked shrimp and mashed potatoes.

★ Indian-Style: Combine chopped fresh mint and mashed potatoes.

2 tablespoons butter, plus more
   to grease
3 medium yellow onions, very
   thinly sliced
2 medium-sized baking
   potatoes, washed thoroughly,
   peeled, and cut crosswise into
   ⅛-inch-thick slices preferably
   using a food processor fitted
   with a slicing disk or a
   mandoline following
   manufacturer's instructions.
   (Note: The slices should be
   thin enough to see the outline
   of the knife through them.)
3 large eggs
1½ cups milk, at room
   temperature
1 tablespoon dry sherry
1 teaspoon dry mustard
¼ teaspoon salt
½ teaspoon freshly ground
   white pepper

1. In a large heavy skillet over medium-high heat, melt the butter. Add the onions and cook, stirring often, for 10 to 12 minutes or until they begin to brown. Cover and cook, stirring once, for 5 to 7 minutes more or until the onion is golden brown. Stir in the potatoes, and cook, uncovered, gently stirring often, for 6 to 8 minutes more until the potatoes are tender. Reserve.

2. Preheat the oven to 375°F. Butter a 2-quart baking dish.

3. In a medium bowl whisk together the eggs, milk, sherry, dry mustard, salt, pepper, and celery seed until well blended. Stir in ½ cup of the Gruyère cheese.

4. Transfer the reserved onion-potato mixture to the bottom of the baking dish and spread evenly. Pour the egg mixture over the onion-potato mixture and sprinkle the remaining ½ cup Gruyère cheese evenly over the top.

5. Bake for 35 to 45 minutes or until set and the top is golden brown. Cut the pudding into squares, sprinkle evenly with the parsley, and serve hot, as an accompaniment to a beef or chicken entrée.

FARMERS' POTATO AND ONION PUDDING

(UNITED STATES)
Serves 4 to 6

½ teaspoon celery seed
1 cup freshly shredded Swiss
   Gruyère cheese, or
   Emmenthaler or Appenzeller
   cheese
1 tablespoon finely chopped
   fresh parsley, to garnish

1 tablespoon safflower oil or
   vegetable oil, plus more to
   grease
1 medium yellow onion, finely
   chopped
½ pound extra-lean ground beef
½ pound lean ground pork
1 tablespoon tomato paste,
   preferably Italian
½ teaspoon ground cayenne
   (red) pepper
½ teaspoon salt
½ teaspoon freshly ground
   pepper
½ cup finely chopped black
   olives, preferably Greek
   Kalamata olives or other
   brine-cured olives
12 cups firmly packed smooth
   mashed potatoes (page 139),
   preferably from purple-fleshed
   Peruvian potatoes (page 132)
6 hard-cooked eggs, cut in half
   crosswise
1 cup finely chopped unsalted
   peanuts

1. In a large heavy skillet over medium-high heat, heat the oil. Add the onion and cook, stirring often, for 3 to 4 minutes or until soft but not browned. Add the ground beef, ground pork, and tomato paste. Cook, stirring often to break up the clumps, for 10 to 12 minutes or until the beef and pork begin to brown. Carefully pour off the fat from the pan. Stir in the cayenne, salt, and pepper. Stir in the olives and cook for 5 minutes more, stirring occasionally.

2. Using 1 firmly packed cup of mashed potatoes per ball, form the mashed potatoes into 12 balls. Using a large spoon, hollow out each ball, so that the walls are ¼ inch thick. Stuff each hollow with 3 tablespoons of the meat mixture, firmly packing it down into the ball. Then insert a hard-cooked egg half into the hole. Seal the hole with the potato mixture, re-forming the ball. Turn the ball over seam side down, and smooth the surface while shaping the ball. Repeat with the remaining potato and meat mixture until you have 12 stuffed potato balls.

3. Preheat the oven to 375°F.

4. Divide the peanuts among the 12 balls, pressing them into the shape of a small circle into the surface of each ball. Repeat with the remaining balls and transfer the balls to a lightly greased baking sheet, placing them 2 inches apart. Bake for 25 to 30 minutes or until the peanuts are light brown. Serve hot as a main course.

PERUVIAN-STYLE STUFFED POTATO BALLS

(PERU)

*Serves 6, 2 balls
per serving*

6 tablespoons (¾ stick) unsalted
   butter, plus ½ teaspoon to
   grease molds

2 tablespoons freshly grated
   Parmesan cheese

6 ounces very small fresh wild
   mushrooms. Choose from:
   chanterelle, cremini, or oyster,
   wiped clean with a damp
   paper towel, cut lengthwise
   into eighths if large

1 cup firmly packed smooth
   mashed potatoes (page 139),
   at room temperature

4 ounces Swiss Gruyère cheese,
   shredded

3½ tablespoons finely chopped
   fresh chives, plus 1 teaspoon
   to garnish

2 teaspoons Dijon-style mustard

1 teaspoon salt

½ teaspoon freshly ground
   white pepper

⅓ cup sifted all-purpose flour

1 cup milk, heated

6 large eggs, separated, at room
   temperature

1 teaspoon fresh lemon juice

1. Preheat the oven to 400°F. Liberally grease the inside and rims of 4 individual (1½-cup) heatproof soufflé molds with the ½ teaspoon butter and arrange on a baking sheet. Sprinkle each with ½ tablespoon Parmesan cheese to coat the bottom and sides evenly. Refrigerate until ready to use.

2. In a small heavy skillet over medium-high heat, melt 2 tablespoons of the butter. Raise the heat to high, add the mushrooms, and sauté just until golden brown, about 3 minutes. Using a slotted spoon, remove 12 of the prettiest mushrooms for garnish and reserve. Transfer the remaining mushrooms along with the mashed potatoes, Gruyère cheese, chives, mustard, salt, and pepper to a large bowl. Gently stir until well blended and reserve.

3. In the skillet over medium heat melt the remaining 4 tablespoons butter. Whisk in the flour and cook, whisking constantly across the bottom and around the sides, for 2 minutes. Do not allow the *roux* to brown. Gradually whisk in the hot milk. Bring to a boil, whisking constantly, and cook for about 2 minutes or until the mixture is as thick as paste. Remove from the heat and whisk in the egg yolks, one at a time, until well blended. Then gently stir the flour-egg mixture into the reserved potato mixture, until well blended.

4. In a medium bowl beat the egg whites and lemon juice until stiff but glossy, not dry or grainy. Stir about one fourth of the whites into the soufflé base until well blended. Working quickly and lightly, fold the remaining beaten egg whites into the lightened base. Spoon the mixture into the prepared chilled soufflé dishes. Immediately return the dishes to the baking sheet and transfer to the rack in the lower third of the oven. Bake the soufflés for 30 to 35 minutes or until puffy and the tops are crisp and golden brown. Divide the 12 reserved mushrooms and 1 teaspoon chives among the soufflés for garnish. Serve at once.

INDIVIDUAL POTATO-CHEESE SOUFFLÉS WITH WILD MUSHROOMS

(FRANCE)

*Makes 4
individual soufflés*

Cake:

2 cups cake flour

1½ cups sugar

1 teaspoon double-acting baking
  powder

1 teaspoon baking soda

1 teaspoon salt

1½ teaspoons ground cinnamon

½ teaspoon ground mace

½ teaspoon ground cloves

¼ teaspoon ground ginger

¼ teaspoon freshly ground pepper

6 medium carrots, cooked until
  very tender and mashed
  (enough to make 1 cup firmly
  packed mashed carrots)

¾ cup corn oil, plus more to grease

4 large eggs, lightly beaten

Frosting:

Makes about 1½ cups

8 ounces cream cheese,
  preferably lowfat "light," at
  room temperature

2 tablespoons unsalted butter, at
  room temperature

1 cup firmly packed mashed
  potatoes (page 139); combine
  with 2 teaspoons water and
  purée in a blender container
  or food processor fitted with a
  metal blade until very smooth

1¼ cups sifted confectioners' sugar

½ teaspoon pure vanilla extract

3 tablespoons fresh orange juice

1 medium carrot, shredded

CARROT-POTATO TEA CAKES

(UNITED STATES)

Makes 12 to 16 individual tea cakes

1. Preheat the oven to 350°F. Lightly grease the bottom of a 13- by 9- by 2-inch baking pan. Line with waxed paper or parchment paper and lightly grease the top of the paper and sides of the pan.

2. To prepare the cake: In a large bowl sift together the cake flour, sugar, baking powder, baking soda, salt, cinnamon, mace, cloves, ginger, and pepper. Add the puréed carrots, oil, and eggs, and beat just until well blended, being careful not to overmix.

3. Pour the mixture into the prepared pan, smoothing the top. Lightly tap the bottom of the pan on the countertop to remove large air bubbles. Bake on the middle rack of the oven for 35 to 40 minutes, or until a toothpick inserted in the center comes out clean.

4. Let the cake cool in the baking pan for 15 minutes. Then carefully invert it onto a cake rack and unmold. Remove the waxed paper or parchment and discard. Let cool completely, about 1 hour.

5. Meanwhile, prepare the frosting: In a medium bowl cream together the cream cheese, butter, and puréed potatoes. Gradually sift in the confectioners' sugar, beating well after each addition, scraping down the side of the bowl as needed, until the frosting is well blended and smooth. Beat in the vanilla and orange juice until well blended and fold in the carrots. Refrigerate until ready to use. (The frosting can be made up to 1 day ahead. Cover and refrigerate.)

6. Transfer the cake to a sheet of waxed paper, carefully sliding it off the rack onto the paper. Using a cookie cutter 3½ inches in diameter in a simple shape (easier to cut cake) of your choice, carefully cut out 12 to 16 pieces of cake as close as possible to one another. (*Note*: The number of portions depends on the shape of the cutter.) Repeat the process until you have 12 to 16 miniature cakes.

7. To serve, brush off any loose crumbs from the surface of the cakes, and frost the top and sides of each miniature cake. Serve at room temperature or chilled. To store: Arrange in a single layer in a large deep pan, cover so as not to disturb the frosting, and refrigerate for up to 2 days.

"Did you know that they (the Inca) measured their units of time by the time it takes a potato to cook?"
—*Jane Grigson,*
Jane Grigson's
Vegetable Book,
1979

Sautéed and Fried

4

BUBBLE AND SQUEAK

2 tablespoons olive oil

1 cup finely chopped onion

2½ cups loosely packed finely
   shredded Savoy or green
   cabbage (about ¼ small
   head)

1½ tablespoons strong coarse
   mustard

2 cups firmly packed smooth
   mashed potatoes (page 139)

1 teaspoon salt

½ teaspoon freshly ground
   pepper

4 ¼-inch-thick slices boiled or
   roasted beef, or roasted pork,
   at room temperature
   (optional)

> "Whenever I fall in love,
> I begin with potatoes."
>
> —Nora Ephron,
> Heartburn

(ENGLAND)

Serves 4

1. In a large heavy skillet over medium-high heat, heat 1 tablespoon of the olive oil. Add the onion and shredded cabbage, and cook, stirring, for 8 to 10 minutes or until lightly browned. Stir in the mustard, mashed potatoes, salt, and pepper until well blended. Using a spatula, spread the mixture into an even, firmly packed, flat "cake." With the spatula, push the edges of the cake up to form a raised edge. Cook about 5 to 7 minutes or until the bottom is golden brown. (*Note:* You will hear the "bubbling" and "squeaking" noise of the ingredients sizzling in the skillet.)

2. Carefully place a heatproof plate on top of the skillet and invert the cake onto the plate. Add the remaining tablespoon of olive oil to coat the skillet. Slide the cake, browned side up, back into the skillet. Cook the second side for 4 to 5 minutes or until golden brown. (*Note:* The center should remain moist.) Using the spatula, transfer the whole cake to a serving platter. Or cut it into 4 wedges, and place each wedge on a slice of beef or pork if desired. Serve at once.

POTATO POTPOURRI

Since 1948, the motto of the Idaho license plate has been Famous Potatoes.

In the 1840's, "potato trap" was slang for the word "mouth."

A potatophile is a person who loves potatoes.

The potato was valued in Europe as an aphrodisiac.

2 tablespoons usli ghee (Indian
    clarified butter — see below) or
    olive oil
1 medium yellow onion, finely chopped
3 cloves garlic, finely chopped
1½ tablespoons freshly grated
    peeled gingerroot
1¼ teaspoons ground cinnamon
1¼ teaspoons ground coriander seed
1 teaspoon ground turmeric
¾ teaspoon ground cumin
½ teaspoon dried hot red chili
    pepper flakes
¼ teaspoon ground cloves
¼ teaspoon ground nutmeg,
    preferably freshly grated
4 medium-sized ripe tomatoes,
    peeled, seeded, and coarsely chopped
4 medium boiling potatoes,
    washed thoroughly, peeled,
    and cut into ½-inch dice
¼ cup canned unsweetened
    coconut milk, not canned
    cream of coconut (available at
    foreign section of supermarket
    or gourmet store)
¾ cup frozen green peas, thawed
Salt and freshly ground pepper to taste
Fresh coriander leaves, to garnish

1. In a large heavy skillet over medium-high heat, heat the *usli ghee*. Add the onion and garlic and cook, stirring, for about 4 minutes or until soft but not browned.

2. Reduce the heat to very low, and stir in the gingerroot, cinnamon, ground coriander seed, turmeric, cumin, chili, cloves, and nutmeg. Cook, stirring, for 2 minutes. Add the tomatoes, and cook, stirring often, for 5 minutes.

3. Raise the heat to medium, and stir in the potatoes and ¾ cup of water. Cook, covered, stirring often, for 20 to 25 minutes or until the potatoes are tender but not mushy. (The recipe can be made up to this point 1 day ahead. Let cool, wrap, and refrigerate. Reheat over very low heat before proceeding with recipe.)

4. Stir in the coconut milk and peas, and cook, uncovered, stirring often, for 3 minutes or until the peas are heated through. Season with salt and pepper. Serve hot, garnished with the fresh coriander. Pass with cooked rice and a selection of Indian condiments.

To make *usli ghee*: In a heavy 2-quart saucepan over low heat, gently melt 1 cup (2 sticks) of diced unsalted butter, stirring occasionally. When a thin layer of white foam forms on the surface (about 10 minutes), simmer for 5 minutes or until the foam subsides. Then simmer for 25 to 35 minutes more, stirring often, until the mixture turns golden brown. Immediately remove the saucepan from the heat, transfer the butter to a heatproof bowl or Pyrex cup, and let stand until the brown solids settle to the bottom.

When the butter is cool enough to handle, strain the butter through a sieve lined with a double layer of cheese-cloth into a heatproof bowl. Allow to cool completely, transfer to an airtight container, and seal. Refrigerate for up to 2 months or freeze up to 6 months. Makes about ¾ cup.

OTATO CURRY

(INDIA)

Serves 4

4 medium-sized boiling
   potatoes, washed thoroughly
   and peeled
1 medium yellow onion
2 large eggs, lightly beaten
1 teaspoon salt
½ teaspoon freshly ground
   white pepper
¼ teaspoon celery seed
½ cup unsalted matzo meal
   (available at supermarket) or
   ½ cup sifted all-purpose flour
2 cups safflower oil or vegetable
   oil
Applesauce, preferably
   homemade, to serve

Latkes

(Jewish Potato Cakes)

(UNITED STATES)
*Serves 4, 3 or 4 (3-inch) cakes
per serving*

POTATO POTPOURRI

Throughout the Roaring Twenties a flapper who was considered sexy was called a "hot potato." Perhaps this was because she was too "hot" to handle. . . .

In Scotland in the year 1728 the potato was forbidden by law since it was not mentioned in the Bible and, therefore, deemed an unholy plant.

The word spud was derived from the English gardening tool called spud, which is used for digging up roots.

Historically, Jewish families less wealthy than others were known to use a potato as a *menorah*—the candelabrum used in the Jewish celebration of Chanukah.

1. Shred the potatoes into long thin strips using the shredding disk of a food processor or the large holes on a 4-sided box grater until you have about 5 firmly packed cups. As you shred the potatoes, completely immerse the shreds in a bowl of cold water to prevent discoloration. Shred the onion and reserve in a separate medium bowl.

2. To the medium bowl with the reserved shredded onion, add the eggs, salt, pepper, celery seed, and matzo meal. Drain the potatoes, and using your hands squeeze out any excess water. Combine the potatoes with the egg mixture, gently stirring them until well blended, but do not overmix.

3. In a large heavy 10-inch skillet over medium-high heat, heat the oil. (*Note*: You should have enough oil to fill the skillet ½ inch deep.) Working quickly, with your hands form 2 heaping tablespoonfuls of the potato mixture into a 3-inch-wide flat pancake, squeezing out excess liquid while you do so. Repeat with the remaining batter until you have 12 to 16 potato cakes. (*Note*: To test the readiness of the oil drop a teaspoon of the batter into the oil; it should take about 30 seconds to brown each side.) Fry the potato cakes in batches of 2 or 3 (do not crowd the skillet) about 3 to 4 minutes per side or until crisp and golden brown. Drain each batch on a paper towel-lined baking sheet. Serve at once with applesauce passed separately.

POTATO POTPOURRI

F.D.A. (United States Food and Drug Administration) surveys show that as of 1990 the average American eats 124 pounds of potatoes per year while the average European consumes twice that much—imagine!

A 1988 F.D.A. survey reports that in America 37 percent of all fresh vegetables consumed are potatoes. For American males from the ages of 12 to 19 years, white potatoes, including fries, account for 49 percent of all vegetables eaten.

During the 1950's "a potato head" meant a stupid, oafish person.

**P**OTATOES PAPRIKASH

112

1 tablespoon unsalted butter

1 medium white onion, finely chopped

1 medium green bell pepper, cored, seeded, and coarsely chopped

1 medium yellow bell pepper, cored, seeded, and coarsely chopped

4 medium-sized boiling potatoes, washed thoroughly, peeled, and cut crosswise into ⅛-inch-thick slices, preferably using a food processor fitted with a slicing disk or a mandoline, following manufacturer's instructions.

1 medium-sized ripe tomato, peeled, cored, seeded, and coarsely chopped

1 cup homemade chicken stock or canned low-sodium chicken broth

1 tablespoon, plus 2 teaspoons, sweet Hungarian paprika

1½ teaspoons caraway seeds

Pinch ground cayenne (red) pepper

Salt and freshly ground pepper to taste

¼ cup sour cream or plain lowfat yogurt, at room temperature, to garnish

Finely chopped fresh parsley, preferably Italian flat-leaf, to garnish

1. In a large heavy skillet over medium-high heat, melt the butter. Add the onion and bell peppers and cook, stirring often, for 6 minutes or just until the peppers are tender.

2. Stir in the potatoes, tomato, chicken stock, paprika, caraway seeds, and cayenne pepper. Bring to a boil, then reduce the heat to low and partially cover. Simmer, stirring occasionally, for 10 to 15 minutes or until the potatoes are soft but not falling apart. Season to taste with salt and pepper. (The recipe can be made up to this point 1 day ahead. Let cool, wrap, and refrigerate. Combine with ½ cup water and reheat gently over very low heat before proceeding with recipe.)

3. Divide the paprikash among 4 bowls. Garnish with a dollop of sour cream, sprinkle with parsley, and serve.

POTATO POTPOURRI

★ On August 25, 1988, Peter Dowdeswell of Earls Barton, England, set the record for eating 3 pounds of potatoes in 1 minute 22 seconds.

★ In February, 1977, Charles Chip, Inc., of Mountville, PA, produced the largest potato chips ever from oversized potatoes. They were 4 by 7 inches.

★ The largest potato was reported on February 17, 1795, from Thomas Seddal's garden in Chester, England. It weighed 18 pounds 4 ounces.

★ On October 18, 1982, Ovid Harrison of Kite, Georgia, produced the largest sweet potato. It weighed 40¾ pounds.

ARATOGA CHIPS

*(Potato chips were once
known in the United States
as "Saratoga Chips,"
named for the New York
horseracing spatown
in which they originated)*

Serves 4

*3 quarts safflower oil, peanut
oil, or corn oil, for deep frying*
*4 medium-sized baking
potatoes, washed thoroughly,
peeled, and cut crosswise into
⅛-inch-thick slices with a
food processor fitted with a
slicing disk or a mandoline,
following manufacturer's
instructions (Or cut into ⅛-
inch-thick waffled slices, using
the mandoline, following
manufacturer's instructions.)*
1 cup cornstarch
Salt to taste (optional)

1. In a heavy 6- to 8-quart pot over medium-high heat, heat the safflower oil until it reads 365°F. on a deep-fry thermometer. To test, drop a potato slice into the oil. If it sizzles, the oil is hot enough.

2. Meanwhile, put the potato slices in a colander and rinse under cold running water. Drain and pat dry while rubbing with paper towels to help remove some of the surface starch. In a large bowl put the cornstarch and the potato slices, and toss together until the slices are evenly coated, shaking off any excess cornstarch.

3. When the oil is ready, lower an empty deep-frying basket into the oil to coat. (*Note*: Be careful—wear flameproof mitts when deep frying.) Then lift it out of the oil, and add a batch of potato slices to the oiled basket. Be careful not to crowd the basket. Lower the basket back into the oil. Deep fry the chips for about 3 minutes or until crisp and lightly golden brown. (*Note*: Be careful not to overcook the chips, as they will continue to cook slightly even after you remove them.) Lift the basket out, holding it over the pot to drain, then empty the basket onto a paper towel-lined baking sheet to drain. Transfer the chips to a baking dish and place in a preheated oven about 200°F. to keep warm.

4. Repeat with the remaining potatoes, transferring them to the warm oven in between batches to keep warm.

5. Just before serving, if liked sprinkle the crisps lightly with salt. Do not salt until just before serving because salt breaks down the oil. Serve hot.

 CARAMELIZED POTATOES

½ cup sugar

2 tablespoons unsalted butter,
  melted

1 tablespoon safflower or
  vegetable oil

16 whole small new potatoes,
  washed thoroughly, peeled,
  steamed just until tender
  (page 136), and patted dry

Freshly ground pepper to taste

(DENMARK)

Serves 4

Place the sugar in a large heavy skillet over medium-low heat. Cook, stirring often with a wooden spoon, for about 5 to 8 minutes or until the sugar melts and comes to a boil. Boil (do not stir) for about 2 to 4 minutes or until the mixture turns golden brown but is still syrupy. Do not allow the caramel to overcook or it will be bitter. Working quickly, stir in the melted butter and safflower oil until well blended. Then stir in the cooked potatoes, shaking the skillet constantly to rotate the potatoes until they are evenly coated with the caramel. Season with pepper and serve at once. Caramelized potatoes complement a main course of roasted lamb or roasted turkey.

POTATO POTPOURRI

According to the 1990 *Guinness Book of World Records*, in May 1969, Paul G. Tully of Brisbane University, Australia, set the record for potato chip consumption. He ate 30 (2-ounce) bags in 24 minutes 33.6 seconds, without a drink.

It takes 5 tons of raw potatoes to make 1 ton of potato chips.

POTATO POTPOURRI

Among the old-fashioned (but still popular) foodstuffs made with potatoes are: potato flour, potato starch, and even potato syrup! Potato syrup was a familiar product in the 1800's that is very sweet and can be used as a substitute for honey.

JALAPEÑO BATTER-FRIED SHOESTRING POTATOES

3 quarts safflower oil, peanut
   oil, or corn oil, for deep frying
3 medium-sized baking
   potatoes, washed thoroughly,
   peeled, and cut lengthwise
   into ⅛-inch julienne strips (as
   thick as a matchstick), made
   as long as possible to resemble
   "shoestrings," by using a
   mandoline and following
   manufacturer's instructions, or
   a food processor fitted with a
   shredding disk, or a rotary
   grater with large-holed drum
2 large eggs, lightly beaten
2 tablespoons skim or whole
   milk
2 to 3 fresh jalapeño peppers
   (depending on hotness
   desired), seeded, ribs removed,
   and minced (page 59)
2 cups yellow cornmeal
3 tablespoons chili powder
Salt to taste (optional)

Ketchup, to serve (optional)

(MEXICO)

Serves 4

1. In a heavy 6- to 8-quart pot over medium-high heat, heat the safflower oil until it reads 375°F. on a deep-fry thermometer. To test, drop a potato shoestring into the oil. If it sizzles the oil is hot enough.

2. Meanwhile, in a large bowl combine the eggs and milk and whisk until well blended. Add the shoestrings and gently stir until well coated. Drain in a colander. Then toss together with the jalapeño until well coated. In another large bowl combine the cornmeal and chili powder. Stir until well blended. Add the shoestrings to the cornmeal mixture and toss until evenly coated. Shake off any excess.

3. When the oil is ready, lower an empty deep-frying basket into the oil to coat. (Note: Be careful—wear flameproof mitts when deep frying.) Then lift it out of the oil, and add a batch of shoestrings to the oiled basket. Be careful not to crowd the pot. Lower the basket back into the oil. Deep fry the shoestrings for 2 or 3 minutes or until crisp and lightly golden brown. (Note: Be careful not to overcook the shoestrings as they will continue to cook slightly even after you remove them.) Lift the basket out, holding it over the pot to drain, then empty the basket onto a paper towel-lined baking sheet to drain briefly. Transfer the potatoes to a baking dish and place in a preheated oven about 200°F. to keep warm until ready to serve.

4. Repeat with the remaining batter-coated shoestrings, skimming the surface in between batches to keep oil clean, draining, then transferring them to the oven in between batches to keep warm until ready to serve.

5. Just before serving, if desired sprinkle the shoestrings with salt. Do not salt before because salt breaks down the oil. Serve hot and pass with ketchup if desired for guests to help themselves.

4 medium-sized baking
potatoes, washed thoroughly
Safflower oil or vegetable oil, to
grease
¼ cup (½ stick) unsalted butter,
melted
1 teaspoon coarse (kosher) salt
1 tablespoon unseasoned dry
bread crumbs
½ teaspoon paprika, preferably
Hungarian semisweet or hot
(Source Lists, page 142), to
garnish

> "Forget caviar and
> candy for once, why
> not give potatoes for
> Christmas?"
> —Lynda Brown, The
> Guardian, 1987

(SWEDEN)

Serves 4

ASSELBACK POTATOES

(Roasted Potatoes)

1. Preheat the oven to 450°F.

2. Peel the potatoes and place them in a bowl of cold water, making sure they are completely immersed to help prevent discoloration while cutting them. Place each potato in the hollow of a deep wooden spoon, large enough to hold the potato firmly so it can be sliced. Beginning ½ inch from one end of the potato, carefully make ⅛-inch-thick slices down the length of the potato just until the knife stops at the rim of the spoon (do not cut all the way through the potato), ending ½ inch from the opposite end.

3. Drain, then pat dry the potatoes with paper towels. Grease the bottom of a 9-inch square baking dish (large enough to hold the potatoes in a single layer) with a little safflower oil. Transfer the potatoes to the dish cut side up. Brush the entire surface of each potato with 1½ teaspoons of the melted butter (a total of 2 tablespoons) and sprinkle the tops with the coarse salt.

4. Roast the potatoes for 40 to 50 minutes or until the potatoes are golden brown and they test tender when pierced with a fork. Remove the baking dish from the oven and sprinkle each potato with the bread crumbs and drizzle with the remaining 2 tablespoons butter (1½ teaspoons per potato). Return the baking dish to the oven and roast for 5 minutes more. Sprinkle paprika in a strip down the center of each potato and serve at once. Hasselback Potatoes complement a main course of pork, fish, chicken, beef, or lamb.

 SECRET INGREDIENT COOKIES

1¼ cups sifted all-purpose flour

¼ teaspoon salt

1¼ teaspoons double-acting baking powder

½ cup (1 stick) unsalted butter, melted

¾ cup sugar

1 large egg, lightly beaten

1 teaspoon pure vanilla extract

¼ teaspoon ground cinnamon

¾ cup crushed unsalted potato chips

2 ounces whole pecan halves, to garnish (optional)

1. Sift together the flour, salt, and baking powder three times. In a medium bowl mix together the melted butter and sugar until well blended. Beat in the egg, vanilla, and cinnamon until well blended.

2. Gradually add the flour mixture to the egg mixture in ¼-cup increments, beating well after each addition. Stir in the potato chips until well blended.

3. Shape the mixture into a roll about 7 inches long and 2 inches in diameter. Wrap the dough roll in waxed paper, sealing the ends tightly. (The recipe can be made up to this point 3 days ahead. Wrap and refrigerate.) Chill in the refrigerator overnight or place in the freezer just until firm and it can be easily sliced.

4. Preheat the oven to 350°F.

5. Unwrap the dough and cut the roll into ¼-inch-thick slices. Arrange on an ungreased baking sheet 1 inch apart. Place a pecan half in the center of each cookie if desired. Bake for 12 to 15 minutes or until the edges are very lightly browned. Serve warm, or transfer to a rack to cool and serve at room temperature. Store in an airtight container or jar for up to 4 days.

★ SPUD SLANG ★

Spud

Lumper

Tater

Earth Apple

Irish Grape

Lunker (large potato)

★ SPUD-EXTRACURRICULAR ACTIVITIES ★
Fun with Potatoes

★ Aroostook County, Maine, July Potato Blossom Festival.

★ Ocean City, New Jersey, hosts an array of annual pageants and contests, including a freckle competition, a bald-spot contest—and yes—a French fry-sculpting competition. Among the entries were a pizza made of french fries (with ketchup posing as sauce) and volcanoes. The list goes on. The winner: "Vampire's Toothbrush," ketchup adorning the "bloody" toothbrush.

★ Potato-wrestling, (The sport of wrestling in staggering amounts of mashed potatoes; most popular is sweet potatoes.)

★ Potato stamp printing. Cut a potato in half lengthwise and using a pen (a pencil won't work on the wet spud) draw a design such as a tree or flower on the cut side of the spud. Using a small, sharp knife cut straight down into the potato to the depth of a ½ inch, tracing the design. Then, holding the knife horizontally, very carefully cut around the design only to the depth of the ½-inch mark, discarding the scraps of potato. Using a paint brush lightly paint the color(s) of your choice on the design, then press the potato stamp to print the design. Be creative—you can print on paper, cloth, or wood.

BLUE RIBBON SWEET POTATO DOUGHNUTS

(UNITED STATES)

*Makes about
2½ dozen 2½-inch doughnuts
and holes*

2 large eggs

½ cup firmly packed light
brown sugar

1 cup firmly packed mashed
sweet potatoes (page 139),
preferably from variety
labeled yams (page 136)

1 cup lowfat buttermilk

3 tablespoons unsalted butter,
melted

½ teaspoon freshly ground
pepper

½ teaspoon freshly ground mace

3½ cups sifted all-purpose flour,
plus more to dust

1 tablespoon double-acting
baking powder

½ teaspoon baking soda

¾ teaspoon salt

3 quarts safflower oil or
vegetable oil, for frying

¼ cup sugar mixed together
with 1 tablespoon ground
cinnamon, to garnish
(optional)

1. In a medium bowl beat together the eggs, brown sugar, mashed sweet potatoes, buttermilk, melted butter, pepper, and mace until well blended.

2. In a separate medium bowl sift together the flour, baking powder, baking soda, and salt.

3. Stir enough of the flour mixture into the egg mixture just until the mixture forms a soft dough, reserving the remainder. Turn out on to a lightly floured work surface and knead for 10 turns working in the remaining flour mixture until the dough is less sticky and is manageable. Pat or roll out the dough to a uniform ½ inch thickness. Cut the dough with a well-floured 2½-inch doughnut cutter. (Or use 2 different-sized biscuit cutters. One should be about 2½ inches in diameter, the other 1 inch for the doughnut hole.) Dip the cutter back into the flour between cuts. Reroll scraps of dough and repeat the process until you have about 2½ dozen doughnuts and holes. Let the doughnuts and holes stand for 10 minutes.

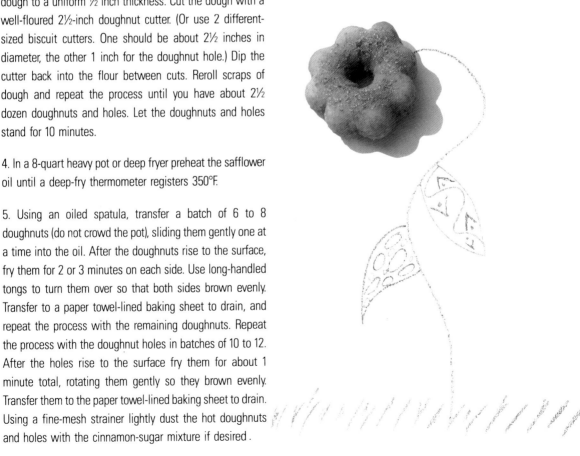

4. In a 8-quart heavy pot or deep fryer preheat the safflower oil until a deep-fry thermometer registers 350°F.

5. Using an oiled spatula, transfer a batch of 6 to 8 doughnuts (do not crowd the pot), sliding them gently one at a time into the oil. After the doughnuts rise to the surface, fry them for 2 or 3 minutes on each side. Use long-handled tongs to turn them over so that both sides brown evenly. Transfer to a paper towel-lined baking sheet to drain, and repeat the process with the remaining doughnuts. Repeat the process with the doughnut holes in batches of 10 to 12. After the holes rise to the surface fry them for about 1 minute total, rotating them gently so they brown evenly. Transfer them to the paper towel-lined baking sheet to drain. Using a fine-mesh strainer lightly dust the hot doughnuts and holes with the cinnamon-sugar mixture if desired .

Sauce:

Makes 1 cup

¾ *cup rice wine vinegar*

¼ *cup "lite" soy sauce*

2 teaspoons freshly grated
*   peeled gingerroot*

1 teaspoon freshly grated
*   orange or lemon zest*

2 cloves garlic, crushed

Tempura:

3 quarts peanut oil, safflower
*   oil, or corn oil, for deep frying*

¼ *teaspoon pure Oriental*
*   sesame oil (optional)*

2 large egg yolks, lightly beaten

1 cup ice water

1 cup cake flour, plus ½ *cup to*
*   dust*

½ *teaspoon double-acting*
*   baking powder*

½ *teaspoon salt*

2 medium sweet potatoes,
*   preferably variety labeled*
*   yams (page 133), boiled until*
*   just tender (page 136), peeled*
*   and cut into* ¹⁄₁₆*-inch-thick*
*   slices*

4 sprigs fresh parsley, preferably
*   Italian flat-leaf, dried well, to*
*   garnish (optional)*

1. To prepare the sauce: In a nonreactive heavy 1-quart saucepan over very low heat, combine the rice wine vinegar, soy sauce, ginger, orange zest, and garlic. Heat gently, stirring occasionally, until ready to serve.

2. To prepare the tempura: In a heavy 6- to 8-quart pot over medium-high heat, heat the peanut oil and sesame oil if desired until it reads 360°F. on a deep-fry thermometer. To test, drop a little batter into the oil. If it sinks then rises to the surface, the oil is hot enough.

3. Meanwhile, in a medium bowl combine the egg yolks, ice water, the 1 cup cake flour, baking powder, and salt. Stir, do not whisk, until just blended (the batter will still be lumpy). Pat dry the sweet potato slices to remove excess moisture. To a medium bowl add the ½ cup cake flour and add the sweet potato slices, tossing together until the slices are evenly coated and shaking off any excess flour.

4. When the oil is ready, with tongs or chopsticks, dip a few of the sweet potato slices into the batter until evenly coated, and using a long-handled wire skimmer or slotted spoon drop the sweet potatoes, one by one, in small batches (do not crowd the pot—the slices should not touch each other)

SWEET POTATO TEMPURA WITH DIPPING SAUCE

(JAPAN)

Serves 4

into the hot oil. (*Note*: Be careful—wear flameproof mitts when deep frying.) Deep fry the sweet potatoes for 1 to 2 minutes or until the edges are light golden brown, then flip over and deep fry the other side for about 1 to 2 minutes more or until puffed, crisp, and light golden brown. (*Note*: Be careful not to overcook the tempura as it will continue to cook slightly even after you remove it.) Transfer the potatoes to a paper towel-lined baking sheet to drain briefly, then to a heated platter to keep warm in between batches.

5. Repeat with the remaining potatoes and batter, skimming the surface of the oil often between batches to keep it clean, and then draining and transferring the tempura to a platter to keep warm until ready to serve.

6. Just before serving, if desired deep fry the parsley sprigs (do not dip in batter) for about 1 second, turning quickly, just until crisp (not browned). Drain briefly on the paper towel-lined baking sheet until ready to serve.

7. To serve, divide the tempura among 4 plates. Garnish each with a fried parsley sprig if desired and accompany with a bowl of hot dipping sauce. Serve at once. Serve as an appetizer or as a side dish.

POTATO POTPOURRI

The potato tuber is the only edible part of the potato plant. The rest, including the flower, is inedible. The potato sprout when eaten in large quantities can be toxic. ★ In the 1980's the phrase "couch potato" meant a person who was a television addict, so intent on watching the T.V. that he or she never moved from the couch. ★ Potatoes can help reduce air pollution since they produce ethanol. ★ According to the U.S. Department of Agriculture, survival is possible on a diet solely of potatoes and whole milk.

¼ cup usli ghee or safflower oil,
   plus more if needed
10 small new potatoes, peeled,
   pricked all over with a fork,
   and quartered; if large cut
   into eighths so all pieces are
   uniform in size, or use a
   melon baller to scoop the flesh
   from 4 large boiling potatoes
   into small balls
1 cup finely chopped onion
1 tablespoon freshly grated
   peeled gingerroot
4 cardamom pods, preferably
   green, shelled, seeds ground
½ teaspoon ground turmeric
½ teaspoon ground cayenne
   (red) pepper
2 teaspoons ground coriander
   seeds
1 teaspoon ground cinnamon
½ teaspoon ground cloves
2 tablespoons fresh lemon juice
½ cup plain lowfat yogurt, at
   room temperature
½ cup freshly grated coconut
   or unsweetened shredded
   coconut, finely chopped
1 teaspoon salt
½ teaspoon freshly ground
   pepper

DUM ALOO

1. In a large heavy skillet or 6- to 8-quart saucepan (large enough to hold the potatoes in a single layer) over medium-high heat, heat 3 tablespoons of the *usli ghee*. Add the potatoes and sauté them, adding more *usli ghee* if needed to coat the skillet, for 12 to 15 minutes, or until they are well browned and test tender when pierced with a fork. Using a slotted spoon, transfer to a heatproof bowl and reserve.

2. Add the remaining 1 tablespoon *usli ghee* to the skillet along with the onion. Sauté the onion for 5 to 7 minutes, or until golden brown.

(INDIA)

Serves 4

(Potatoes in Spicy
Yogurt Sauce)

3. Reduce the heat to medium and stir in the ginger, cardamom pods, turmeric, cayenne, ground coriander, cinnamon, cloves, and lemon juice, stirring vigorously for 10 seconds. Reduce the heat to low and stir in the yogurt, coconut, salt, and pepper until well blended. Bring to a boil. Add the reserved potatoes and cook for 5 minutes, stirring often. (*Note*: If the sauce is too thick, stir in a few tablespoons water until desired consistency is reached.) Serve at once. (This recipe is best when made at least 4 hours in advance or up to 2 days ahead. Let cool, wrap, and refrigerate. Reheat over low heat before serving.)

A Healthful Note to the Reader

My goal has been to create recipes featuring the potato that are healthful and that are conservative with the use of fat, sugar, and salt without forsaking flavor. I have not completely avoided ingredients like butter, milk, eggs, sugar, and salt since in many instances these are necessary to maintain the integrity and particular flavor of a traditional ethnic recipe. I have, however, assuredly reduced the amount of less healthful ingredients, making the collection of recipes more "health-wise."

Here are simple ways in which you can make recipes health-wise:

★ Use whole milk in place of beaten egg for glazes on baked goods.

★ Rinse and drain oil-packed or brine-packed foods like anchovies, beans, olives, and capers before using.

★ Trim meats and poultry of excess fat.

★ Whenever possible, keep vegetable and fruit skins intact; this is where most of the nutrients are contained.

★ Use nonstick cookware. It allows you to use less fat in cooking; in some cases, none at all, as with an omelet. Another bonus: nonstick cookware is easier to wash!

★ When shopping, read all labels carefully. Nutritionally "modified" products are not always what they seem. For example, "light" or "lite" may actually refer to the taste or consistency of a product. Claims can be ambiguous—calories and fat content might be the same! Also, make sure that after being modified the product is still nutritious!

★ In many of the recipes I have included page references that will answer any questions you might have.

They may direct you to a quick cooking method, such as for boiling potatoes, or to a concise summary of the differences among potato types, such as the hard-to-decipher myth between yams and sweet potatoes. In other cases the reference is to a tip on the preparation of an ingredient — how to grate fresh coconut or seed a jalapeño pepper, for example. And in a few instances I direct you to Source Lists in the event you want to order by mail an item that you cannot find in your area.

Even though there are many species of white potatoes, they can be categorized into the four basic kinds found at your supermarket. If you want to try different varieties — purple-fleshed, yellow-fleshed, and the like — try gourmet stores and health-food markets, or Mail-Order Source Lists (page 142). You can also call the office of your state agricultural department for a list of farmers' markets near you.

RUSSETS These are "mealy" brown- and rough-skinned, oblong, *baking potatoes* whose skin has a net-like appearance. No matter where this potato is grown, it is known as the "Idaho potato." The eyes are prominent.

LONG WHITES These are off-yellow ("fawn") in color, elliptical in shape, smooth in texture, thin-skinned *all-purpose potatoes*. The eyes are barely detectable.

ROUND WHITES These are creamy-beige in color, "waxy," round, smooth, fairly thin-skinned *boiling potatoes*.

ROUND REDS These are "waxy," round, smooth, fairly thin-skinned dark-red *boiling potatoes* that can be round to oblong in shape.

BASIC TYPES

The four kinds of potatoes above are referred to as either "waxy" or "mealy." Waxy potatoes are lower in starch and have a waxy, moist interior. Potatoes described as "mealy" are high in starch and have a drier mealy or floury interior. These terms are useful for determining how to prepare potatoes. How a potato cooks depends upon its starch content. Waxy potatoes contain more liquid; they keep their shape, therefore, when cooked and do not absorb as much liquid when added to a soup or salad. Mealy potatoes are great for mashed or baked potatoes because they have a fluffier texture when cooked.

In this book I go further in distinguishing which type of potato to use in each recipe. Since a waxy potato is best for boiling, I refer to them as "boiling" potatoes. Mealy potatoes are best for baking, and throughout when needed I call for "baking" potatoes. This method makes it much easier to prepare your shopping list for any given recipe, as boiling and baking are the most commonly used terms at supermarkets.

In sum, waxy potatoes are good for cooking techniques wherein the potatoes need to hold their shape, such as boiling, steaming, roasting, and sautéeing. Round Whites and Round Reds are waxy potatoes.

Mealy potatoes are good for cooking techniques wherein it doesn't matter if the potato keeps its shape, such as baking, mashing (or for mashed potatoes to be used as an ingredient in baked goods), puréeing, and deep frying. Russet potatoes belong to this category. The wonderfully thin-skinned Long White potato can be considered all-purpose. If you are at the market and don't know what dish you will be preparing — do you need boiling or baking potatoes? — this all-purpose one can help you out of a bind, though, alas, it is not always in stock.

TATER TEST

If you have a hard time deciding whether a potato is waxy (best for boiling) or mealy (best for baking), use the following test, based on Harold McGee's *On Food and Cooking*, to establish type.

Make a solution of 2 parts water to 1 part salt. Add the potato. If it is waxy it will float; if mealy it will sink.

KNOWING THE NEW POTATO

New potatoes are not a separate kind of potato, but rather any freshly dug potato that has not reached maturity. Size, variety, and type (waxy or mealy) are irrelevant. True new potatoes are sold from late winter or early spring through midsummer. Everyone prefers the smallest ones possible ("peewees"), as they are slightly sweet (not all the sugar has turned to starch yet). They are a gastronomic treat, not to be missed! A new potato hasn't fully developed its skin yet either, so if you are unsure whether or not it is a freshly dug potato, just rub it with your thumb. If the skin is thin and flakes easily, it is most certainly a new potato.

When preparing new potatoes, don't scrub them, just gently wipe the delicate skin clean with a damp paper towel before cooking. They are also quite perishable, so use them quickly. Since their flesh is moist and waxy, they are at their very best unpeeled and roasted, steamed, or boiled.

SWEET POTATOES VERSUS YAMS

Even though the sweet potato can be substituted for the potato in any recipe, technically the sweet potato is *not* a potato. The sweet potato (*Ipomoea batata*) is a member of the morning glory family, whereas the potato (*Solanum tuberosum*) belongs to the nightshade family.

The sweet potato has varieties whose skin ranges from pinkish to reddish brown in color and flesh yellowish white to deep orange. True yams are difficult to find in American supermarkets (even canned "candied yams" are really sweet potatoes — read the list of ingredients!). Most grocers mistakenly label a deep-orange fleshed sweet potato as a yam. Most of the recipes in this book that call for sweet potatoes ask for "the variety labeled yams," referring to this darker-skinned, deep orange–fleshed variety of sweet potato. This sweet potato is sweeter and moister than the "pale" sweet potato with yellow flesh.

Sweet potatoes are not related to the true "yam" (*Dioscorea bulbifera*), which grows on a tropical climbing vine. If you want to try genuine yams you can sometimes find them in markets outside the tropics, particularly vendors that carry Caribbean or Latin produce and wares.

THE POTATO BIN

Before embarking on the recipes in this book, it's a good idea to familiarize yourself with general preparation and cooking methods that are used for both potatoes and sweet potatoes.

SELECTING SPUDS Peeled and/or cut potatoes discolor (darken) when exposed to the air. Though this isn't harmful, it is unsightly and is easily avoided. When peeling or cutting potatoes, have a bowl of cold water on hand. As you work add the potatoes to the bowl of water,

making sure they are completely immersed. When ready to proceed with the recipe, drain the potatoes well and blot them dry with paper towels to remove the surface starch and to prevent splattering when cooking in grease.

Avoid green-tinged white potatoes altogether; green spots or green-tinged flesh are an indication of solanine, which in small quantities can make you feel ill — in large doses it is poisonous. Exposure to strong light causes potato flesh to turn green so store potatoes in a dark place. Don't try to cut the green flesh away, simply discard the entire potato.

The "eyes" of a potato each have a bud underneath, from which a sprout grows into a mature plant. If a potato has sprouted, throw it away. Don't bother to cut away the sprouts because the potato won't be tasty anyway. Also, sprouts on a potato, when eaten in large quantity, can be harmful.

Cooking the Perfect Potato

YIELD Naturally the recipe you use will state the number of servings. However, if you are ad-libbing, here are some guidelines:

1 medium potato or 1 small sweet potato = 1 serving
4 small new potatoes = 1 serving
6 very small new potatoes = 1 serving
1 medium-sized cooked potato or 1 small cooked sweet potato = ½ cup firmly packed mashed

BOILING

1. Use only the "boiling" type of potatoes (page 132) for boiling, unless making mashed potatoes, when you should boil the "baking" type of potato (page 132). Gently scrub whole potatoes under cold running water until clean and don't peel them before boiling. The potato skin is a natural envelope that seals in flavor and moistness. (The skin is also very nutritious.) In a heavy pot over medium heat, add the "baking" style potatoes and cover with cold water by about 2 inches, and bring to a boil. You can add 1 teaspoon of salt per quart of water, before bringing to a boil, but this is optional. Then reduce the heat to low and simmer, partially covered, for 15 to 25 minutes depending on the size of the potatoes and the quantity in the pot.

2. If boiling new potatoes, immerse them into already boiling water and follow the directions above, but cook for 10 to 15 minutes, again depending on the size of the potatoes and quantity in the pot. (*Note*: It is also a nice touch to boil potatoes in homemade stock.)

3. When the potatoes test tender when the thickest one is pierced in the center with a fork, drain in a colander at once. If the potatoes are to be used in a salad, refresh them under cold running water and proceed with the recipe. If they are to be served warm, cover gently with a clean kitchen towel to keep warm until ready to serve or proceed with the recipe. If you are to be peeling and/or mashing the potatoes, this is easiest to do if the potatoes are warm. Just let them cool enough to handle.

STEAMING

Because of their waxy texture, it is preferable to only steam "boiling" style potatoes (page 15). Gently scrub the potatoes under cold running water and place unpeeled or peeled potatoes directly on a rack or in a steamer basket in a heavy pot over 2 inches of boiling water (the water level should not touch the bottom of the rack or basket). Cover the pot and steam the potatoes for 15 to 30 minutes, depending on the size of the potatoes and quantity in the pot. Steaming times will be longer than those for boiling. Also, you may have to add a little more boiling water halfway through the cooking process. Proceed with step #3 as directed above.

AROMATIC STEAMING LIQUID To really make your potatoes special, add aromatic seasonings, such as garlic, fresh or dried herbs, or spices — allspice or juniper berries, cinnamon sticks or peppercorns — fresh gingerroot, or citrus peels, and so forth to the steaming water. The vapor will impart a subtle, but noticeable flavor to the potatoes. I have also experimented with using fresh vegetable or fruit juices. Homemade vegetable or seafood stocks work wonderfully, as do wine or other liquor-spiked liquids.

BAKING

1. Use only the "baking" type of potato (page 132), the Idaho Russet, for baking unless otherwise directed in a recipe. Preheat the oven to 450°F. Gently scrub the potato clean under cold running water and then pat dry with paper towels (do not peel). Using a skewer or slim-tined fork, pierce the potato in several places. Bake the potato directly on the oven rack for 35 to 45 minutes (depending on the size of the potato and if it is sharing the oven with other dishes), or until the middle of the thickest potato feels soft when squeezed (through a potholder!) with your fingers. If you can, bake only 4 to 6 medium potatoes per oven rack. Also, try not to place the potatoes close to one another or other dishes as this will reduce the crunchiness of the skin. (*Note*: The

longer you bake the potato the better. If you like a very crisp skin and fluffy center, bake up to 1¼ hours, sometimes even longer, depending on desired doneness of the skin.) Don't wrap the potato in foil or the skin will be soggy and the potato mushy in texture. If you want a soft skin, instead of a crisp skin, then rub the potato with a little butter or oil before baking.

I don't recommend using the microwave for "baking" a potato as it really steams it, resulting in a soggy skin. If time is not a factor and your reason for using the microwave to bake a potato is simply that you don't want to heat up a large oven, then I recommend a toaster oven over a microwave.

TOPPINGS Baked potatoes are the prize, the benchmark of potato cookery. A baked potato with an appropriate topping can be an entire meal! It is fun to create themes with potato toppings, such as Cowboy-Style (*chili con carne* with shredded Monterey Jack cheese) or Chinese-Style (your favorite meat or vegetable stir-fry, garnished with crunchy deep-fried noodles.) Always try to use lowfat, reduced calorie, and low-sodium staples, such as lowfat cottage cheese, lowfat plain yogurt, and reduced-sodium Dijon mustard.

ROASTING

1. To roast is to bake in an uncovered pan with dry heat, producing a crisp, dark exterior and a moist interior. Roasting works especially well with small unpeeled new potatoes or larger unpeeled boiling potatoes that can be quartered, sliced, or cut into large cubes. Preheat the oven to 375°F. Gently scrub the potatoes under cold running water and pat dry with paper towels or wash and cut large potatoes accordingly. Transfer the potatoes to a roasting pan (large enough to hold the

potatoes in a single layer) and lightly coat with olive oil or vegetable oil, or dot with butter. Add your favorite seasonings to taste — fresh or dried herbs (rosemary is always a favorite) or peeled garlic cloves — or place the potatoes on a bed of thinly sliced onions sprinkled with paprika. Salt and freshly ground pepper are welcome. Roast, tossing occasionally to baste with oil, for 35 to 45 minutes (depending on size of potatoes and quantity in pan), or until the potatoes test tender when the thickest one is pierced in the center with a fork. Serve hot.

MASHING

1. This is not really a cooking method, as the potatoes have already been boiled or steamed. Use the "baking" type of potatoes; they make a fluffier-textured mashed potato. I don't recommend baking or roasting the potatoes (the dry-heat cooking method) before mashing as the texture of the final dish of mashed potatoes is not as smooth. However, if the mashed potatoes are to be used as an ingredient for baked goods in cakes or breads, it is preferable to bake the potatoes first, rather than boil or steam them. The lower water content makes for a better-textured bread, cake, or cookie.

2. To mash, I suggest an old-fashioned potato masher or large fork. Mash the warm peeled potatoes in up-and-down movements to incorporate as much air as possible and to give a lighter consistency, not sideways or in a circular movement. The motion is very important. (Please don't use a food processor, blender, or electric beater to mash — the result will be glue.) Use a fork or spoon to blend in your choice of embellishments to enrich the mashed potatoes. Serve at once, or, if you must, keep warm in a heatproof, partially covered bowl or in a partially covered upper pan of a double boiler set over warm (not simmering or boiling) water.

SAUTÉING AND SHALLOW AND DEEP FRYING

—Always blot potatoes dry with paper towels before sautéing or frying to prevent them from splattering in the hot fat. They will still make a "sputter" noise, but should not make the oil actually splatter.

—When sautéing or shallow frying, heat the pan first, then add the oil to heat it. The rule is: Add cold oil to a hot pan.

—When sautéing or shallow or deep frying do not crowd the pan. Cook the food in batches and always cut it into uniform pieces for even cooking.

—When frying be cautious and protect yourself from burns with flameproof mitts and long-handled tongs.

—For frying, avoid oils sold as "salad oils." I suggest using safflower oil, because it stands up well to high temperatures. However, if you want flavor, use corn or peanut oil.

—Do not use oil with an altered scent or taste. It usually indicates it has become rancid.

TO AVOID POTENTIALLY DANGEROUS SPLATTERING

For shallow frying, add oil to a depth of about ¼ inch depending on the recipe instructions, but make sure the pan isn't more than ¼ full. When adding oil to a pot for deep frying, add enough to immerse the food, but don't fill the pot more than half full.

—For shallow frying, use a wide shallow heavy pan. For deep frying, use a heavy pot, deeper than it is wide.

—I don't recommend reusing oils after frying because the smoking point will be lower each time it is used and the flavor is never as good. If thriftiness is your motive, choose a less expensive oil.

GRILLING

Try grilling whole baking potatoes instead of baking. Lightly coat the unpeeled baking potatoes with oil, and place on a grill rack. Grill over medium-hot coals, with the lid closed, rotating the potatoes occasionally, for 45 to 60 minutes (depending on the size of the potatoes and the quantity of food on the grill rack).

Or, if you want grilled sliced boiling potatoes, parboil peeled potatoes until just tender. Cut them crosswise into ½-inch-thick slices, lightly coat with oil, and grill about 3 minutes per side, just to heat through and achieve grill marks for a pretty presentation.

Some other ideas: Shish-Kebabs: Parboil unpeeled whole new potatoes until tender, lightly rub with oil, thread on to skewers, and proceed with a kebab recipe. Try grilling potato skins for a snack: Use scooped-out baking potato skins left over from making mashed potatoes. Fold each skin in half lengthwise, lightly coat with oil, and place on grill rack. Grill, flipping once, until the skins are crispy. Don't forget that you can use aromatic wood chips such as hickory, mesquite, and apple wood, or grapevine twigs in the fire to add extra pizazz to your potatoes. Follow the manufacturer's instructions for your grill.

THE MICROWAVE If you want to preserve the purple flesh of the purple, black, or blue variety of potatoes, the microwave does a superb job. The microwave is not my personal choice of cooking method. If you want a cooked potato with a soft skin and a moist, creamy texture (versus a potato with a crisp skin and fluffy texture from baking or roasting) then I recommend steaming because it produces a better-textured potato.

If it is a hot day and time is an issue, follow the manufacturer's guidelines for cooking potatoes, as I find each microwave varies greatly.

POTATOPHILE SOURCE LISTS

POTATOES AND SEED POTATOES

BECKERS SEED POTATOES
R.R. #1
Trout Creek, Ontario POH 2LO
Canada

NEW PENNY FARM
85 Williams Road
Presque Isle, ME 04769
207-768-7551

RONNIGER'S SEED POTATOES
Star Route
Moyie Springs, ID 83845

WALNUT ACRES
Penns Creek, PA 17862
800-433-3998

WOOD PRAIRIE FARM
RFD 1, P.O. Box 164
Bridgewater, ME 04735
800-829-9765

RETAIL STORES FOR POTATOES, KITCHEN TOOLS, AND BOOKS

BRIDGE KITCHENWARE
214 East 52nd Street
New York, NY 10022
212-688-4220
Giant selection of cookware, pastry equipment and other specialized kitchen tools.

EL GALINDO, INC.
1601 East 6th Street
Austin, TX 78702
In Texas
512-478-5756
Outside of Texas
800-447-8905

Many types of fresh tortillas and tortilla chips. Also, 30 types of peppers and a generous variety of salsas.

FOOD OF ALL NATIONS
2121 Ivy Road
Charlottesville, VA 22903
804-296-6131
Large selection of international staples and seasonings. They publish a monthly newsletter.

J.B. PRINCE COMPANY
29 West 38th Street
New York, NY 10018
212-302-8611
A showroom located in New York City boasts a very professional selection of international cooking equipment. Several types of mandolines available. Books geared to the food professional.

HERBS AND SPICES

APHRODISIA PRODUCTS
282 Bleecker Street
New York, NY 10014
212-989-6440
Wide selection of dried herbs and spices. Bulk orders of seasonings available at wholesale prices.

HOUSE OF SPICES
76-17 Broadway
Jackson Heights, NY 11373
718-476-1577
A tremendous selection of Indian and Pakistani utensils, herbs, and foodstuffs.

PAPRIKAS WEISS IMPORTER
1546 Second Avenue
New York, NY 10028
212-288-6117
The store for Hungarian paprika, available in different strengths. Other Hungarian products and gourmet goods offered.

SPICE MERCHANT
P.O. Box 524
Jackson Hole, WY 83001
307-733-7811
800-551-5999
Chinese, Japanese, Thai, Indonesian, and Vietnamese seasonings and condiments.

MISCELLANEOUS

SEED SAVERS EXCHANGE
R.R. 3, Box 239
Decorah, IA 52101
Members include farmers and serious gardeners dedicated to saving seeds of heirloom vegetables and plants to protect and maintain unusual varieties for future generations.

WORLD FOOD MUSEUM
THE POTATO MUSEUM
P.O. Box 791
Great Falls, VA 22066
The Potato Museum publishes an illustrated newsletter Peelings, just on potatoes, available at a modest fee.

INDEX